IRELAND
BY BIKE™

IRELAND BY BIKE™

21 TOURS GEARED FOR DISCOVERY

SECOND EDITION

ROBIN KRAUSE

THE
MOUNTAINEERS

Published by
The Mountaineers
1001 SW Klickitat Way, Suite 201
Seattle, WA 98134

First edition, 1993; second edition, 1999

Published simultaneously in Great Britain by Cordee, 3a DeMontfort Street, Leicester, England, LE1 7HD

Manufactured in Canada

Edited by Christine Duell
Maps by Robin Krause
All photographs by Robin Krause, unless otherwise noted
Cover and book design by Jennifer Shontz
Layout by Jennifer Shontz

Cover photograph: *Clifden cottage along Sky-Road, County Galway, Ireland*
© Edmund Nagele
Frontispiece: *Kell's Priory near Kilkenny, an ancient complex of massive stone ruins, is quite ignored by most tourists.*

Library of Congress Cataloging-in-Publication Data
Krause, Robin.
    Ireland by bike : 21 tours geared for discovery / Robin Krause. —
2nd ed.
      p.   cm.
    Includes bibliographical references (p. 184–5) and index.
    ISBN 0-89886-622-7
    1. Bicycle touring—Ireland—Guidebooks. 2. Ireland—Guidebooks.
I. Title.
GV1046.I73K73 1999
914.1504'824—dc21   98-53384
                                                   CIP

The second edition of this book is for my wife, Kelly, who suggested our first cycling trip to Ireland. It is also for our two sons, Joel and Conor, who helped make our most recent trip more challenging, eventful, and definitely more fun.

Special thanks also to Kenny, Kim, Trevor, Kayla, and Clint for cycling with us and for their assistance in collecting material for this new edition. To Jay Denker and Jeff Kirchhoff, thanks for their help with the production of route maps and photographs, respectively.

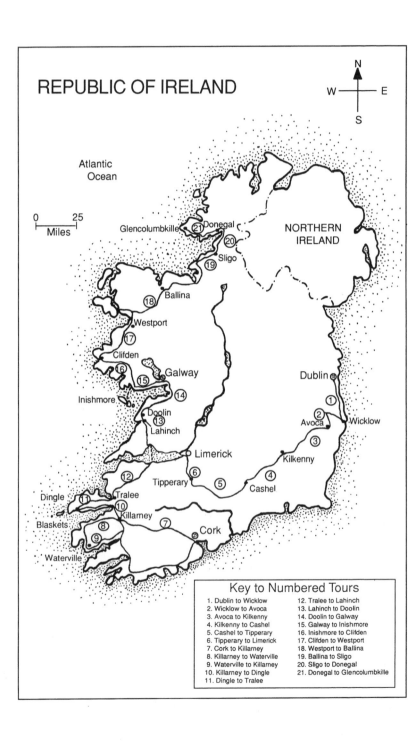

REPUBLIC OF IRELAND

N
W ✦ E
S

Atlantic
Ocean

0   25
Miles

Glencolumbkille ㉑ Donegal
NORTHERN
IRELAND
㉒
Sligo
⑲

Ballina
⑱

Westport
⑰
Clifden
⑯
Galway
⑮
Inishmore
⑭
Doolin
⑬
Lahinch

Dublin
①
②
Avoca   Wicklow
③
Limerick
⑥   Kilkenny
Tipperary   ⑤   ④
⑫   Cashel
Dingle
⑪   Tralee
⑩
Killarney
Blaskets   ⑧   ⑦   Cork
⑨
Waterville

Key to Numbered Tours

1. Dublin to Wicklow
2. Wicklow to Avoca
3. Avoca to Kilkenny
4. Kilkenny to Cashel
5. Cashel to Tipperary
6. Tipperary to Limerick
7. Cork to Killarney
8. Killarney to Waterville
9. Waterville to Killarney
10. Killarney to Dingle
11. Dingle to Tralee

12. Tralee to Lahinch
13. Lahinch to Doolin
14. Doolin to Galway
15. Galway to Inishmore
16. Inishmore to Clifden
17. Clifden to Westport
18. Westport to Ballina
19. Ballina to Sligo
20. Sligo to Donegal
21. Donegal to Glencolumbkille

CONTENTS

A snack break in a small town brings the local kids out to ham it up for the camera.

PREFACE

Nearly fifteen years ago, on a whim, my wife, fellow backpackers, and I decided to use our Eurail Passes to take an overnight ferry from France to Ireland, instead of continuing our trek along the European coast. This casual decision came at the tail end of a whirlwind backpacking trip, and set the stage for what would become three (and counting) lengthy return trips to Ireland.

Not knowing what to expect, I distinctly remember leaving the boat and hopping into the car of a bed and breakfast owner, on the wrong side—in the driver's seat—not thinking about the change from right hand to left hand driving. That first day was a flood of new impressions: the lilting Irish accent, the friendliness of the people, and the breathtakingly green countryside.

Since writing a guidebook had never crossed my mind at the time, my record of that first trip consists of only flashes of memory, some photos, and a few notes scribbled on the backs of postcards. But I can still see and feel the warm fire in the Irish pub the night we disembarked in Rosslare Harbour; the bitter, creamy taste of my first draught of Guinness; and one of our hitchhiking forays, which ended with a friendly driver taking my wife and me on a car tour of several traditionally thatched homes.

Unfortunately we had left little time to explore this tiny island, so the trip was confined to parts of the east coast. Our plane had hardly taken off for home before we began formulating plans for a return. While in Ireland we had noticed the relatively uncrowded roads, the beautiful landscape, and the wealth of places to stay. All of those elements suggested that a bicycle would be the perfect way to get around and we had settled on it before we landed back in New York.

Two years later, maps in hand and panniers by our side, my wife and I landed in Cork and began a month-and-a-half-long tour up the west coast and over to Dublin and the east. Our experiences with friendly people and gorgeous scenery multiplied. In Cork we were welcomed by Mrs. O'Mahony who stuffed us with tea and biscuits (cookies) almost the minute we walked in the door of her bed and breakfast. Farther along, John and Anne Sims from Doolin took us in, washed our clothes, and even gave us a lift to the pub when it got too dark to cycle. Numerous others along the way not only shared their homes but welcomed us in conversation, recommended places to stay, and kept our fuel tanks full with homemade scones, hot tea, and biscuits.

Recently we found ourselves sitting in the Dublin Airport lounge, a third cycling trip to Ireland nearing completion. This time it had been another month-and-a-half-long trip, and we had arrived with some high expectations. As our travels took us to familiar places and to cities we had never seen before, we experienced new examples of Irish generosity and saw even more captivating places. One day, near Limerick, our rain-soaked crew was welcomed in from a particularly miserable day by the Nashes. The couple entertained us all day with helpful travel suggestions and plenty of hot tea.

Over the years, "progress" has widened and straightened many of the scenic country backroads, and four-lane highways have became more common than they were on our first visit. Large supermarkets have popped up, even in relatively small towns, and have sometimes crowded out the smaller fresh fruit and vegetable markets and the local butchers. In cities like Galway and Dublin, shopping malls have slowly begun to replace the small "mom and pop" operations much as they have in the United States.

Despite the tendency for the modernization and commercialism that has sprung up, the Ireland of green scenery, unspoiled historic sites, and uncommonly friendly people has yet to offer any real disappointments. Indeed, I can't think of anywhere in the world I'd rather go.

■ ■

PART I

IRELAND BY BIKE

A narrow "boreen," or lane, makes for perfect, uncrowded cycling. Photo by
Jeff Kirchhoff

IRELAND: THE CYCLIST'S POT O' GOLD

There are many reasons Ireland is the perfect choice for someone wanting the excitement and adventure of travel by bike. As you read on, I hope you will see what a good combination bicycling and Ireland make.

Certainly the fact that this truly is the "Emerald Isle," and that "forty shades of green" is really not an exaggeration, is at least some justification for going. Picture yourself pedaling along the coast, a slightly salty breeze in your face. Up ahead a lush green mountain is just beginning to lose its peak to a veil of fog. Off to your right two men turn newly mown hay to dry in a field that plunges down to the sea. Turning into the lane on the left, a farmer walks his half-dozen cattle back to their home pasture while a dog nips at the hooves of the slow or lazy. Or find yourself pulled up to a table in a roadside pub, sipping an Irish brew, and relaxing after a day's ride. The warm smell of burning peat from the fireplace mixes with the voice of the pub's singer to lull you into a daydream about the tastes, roads, and sights you have witnessed during the trip.

The charm of Ireland is found in such experiences, and these are by no means rare or unusual events. Though there are some large cities that offer the standard fare of big city life, most of Ireland is still vitally connected to the land and is thus a fairly rural country still rooted in an agricultural base. Though more than half of the population lives in urban areas, small villages and towns are scattered throughout the country, and many of them have retained their foundations in the rocky soil. This means that such trappings of modern society as traffic jams, fast food, and billboards are the exception rather than the rule. And yet there is much more to the picturesque landscape than is visible on the surface.

Even with all of its impressive beauty, Ireland would be just another island without the sincere affability and general thoughtfulness of the Irish people. Though I have little Irish blood in my ancestry, I am still drawn to this tiny country. The slow pace of life, the warm, genuine conversations, and the feel of being welcome all combine to coax me to go back. And even though the Irish are sometimes resentful of being characterized by the traditional stereotypes, even Irish Tourist Board publications emphasize that "Irish people are naturally hospitable and friendly souls." Though it is impossible for an outsider to comprehend the full meaning of Irishness, I believe that cyclists, because of their slower, more deliberate pace, have an advantage over automobile travelers. If you are going to experience a country that is deeply rooted to the land, then you have to linger and experience the landscape at some speed that allows more than a motor-powered blur.

The island's scant dimensions are ideal for the cyclist. No matter where you are, you're never more than 70 miles from the coast. Seeing the sights is also easy in Ireland, where 15 to 20 miles in any direction may take you from an oyster tavern to precipitous limestone cliffs or a lovely village nestled along the Atlantic.

It will be a long trip indeed if you have to travel more than 30 or 40 miles to see entirely new scenery.

For the type of on-again, off-again, start-and-stop traveling the surroundings require, the pace of the bicycle is beyond compare. Though a few opportunities may be missed as you whiz down a steep hill, cycling provides an excellent compromise between freedom of movement and the fast-paced travel of car or bus. This guidebook can show you how to have a "cycling vacation," two words I believe should be treated as equals.

Because you have chosen to tour by bike you are no doubt a person who wants exercise as well as recreation from this trip. However, don't forget that this is also supposed to be a vacation. Take time to see the sights, talk to people, stop in pubs, visit markets, and the like. Don't feel as though you have to ride all the time. The distances from one tour stop to the next are relatively short, so you should have plenty of time to see the sights when you arrive at the day's destination.

This may be the only chance you'll ever get to visit this special country, so you certainly want to make the most of your visit. If there are sights you want to see but don't have time to ride to, then rent a car, take a bus, or hop on a train. Granted, a bike is the best means of transportation, but it doesn't necessarily have to be your only one. Keep in mind that this is supposed to be a holiday.

This book is designed to be a detailed source of everything from roads and distances to traditional pubs, sights, attractions, and entertainment. Still, you'll want to check out the tourist offices along the way and read Tourist Board publications. Sights along the routes in this book are covered thoroughly but you'll likely want more details on many attractions. In the larger cities such as Dublin, Cork, and Galway, considerable space is given to the specific features that are unique to those areas. On routes between cities, interesting monuments, castles, beaches, and vistas are listed with directions for getting to them.

Tour distances are listed in two ways. The number of miles since the last stop or attraction is given, and the total trip distance on the tour is printed next to that in parentheses. For example, you may read the following statement: "From the crossroad, the church is 2 miles (18.5) away." The "18.5" indicates how many miles since the tour began. Besides distances and road signs, other items of consequence to cyclists are incorporated in the pretrip sections of the book to make the logistics of going to and getting around Ireland much easier. Included are pointers on articles to pack and how to pack them and information about terrain, weather, currency exchange, and so on.

The tours are organized essentially in a clockwise direction. Because the entire loop is more or less circuitous, it is possible to start at any point and find information about connecting trips on either side. You need only check the previous or next tour description. Whether you go for two weeks or two months, there will likely be a route for you. The tours cover many of Ireland's most scenic

Even cab drivers find bikes a useful way to get to work.

places, including the west and southwest, the Dublin region and the east coast, the midlands and Shannonside.

It's also possible to use the train system to go from one point to another. While the rail network is not as complete as it is in other parts of Europe, this is a good way to go from one major city or destination to the next. Bicycles are easily accepted on trains and the price is reasonable. Because of space limitations it's a little more difficult to transport your bike by bus but it can be done, especially in a pinch.

Though designed primarily for self-contained riders, the "Advance Planning" section and the information in the "From Pounds to Pubs: A Taste of Everything Irish" section on weather, language, currency, and other useful items can benefit anyone taking an escorted or van-supported tour as well. The tour sections may alert you to sights and attractions beyond those included in your tour package. In addition, the "Itineraries" section will help you make decisions about which tours to take, especially if you have fairly limited vacation time.

Each tour is arranged to make it useful when arriving at your destination. In larger towns, I first provide a section about the area's history, population, and the like. The next section notes the whereabouts of such amenities as tourist offices, main streets, and bike shops. Once you are oriented, the paragraphs about sights and entertainment tell of local attractions, historic sites, and theaters, as well as where to shop for bargains or souvenirs. And because Ireland is a country of short distances, suggested daytrips are incorporated into the bigger-city tours or where warranted.

With Ireland's charm and seemingly endless scenery and history, it's impossible to chronicle everything you will or should see. In fact, as a cyclist and someone obviously not ready for a "It's Tuesday so this must be Dublin" tour on a diesel-guzzling luxury liner, you probably don't want everything spelled out in black and white. Seeking obscure villages and climbing on unmarked stone ruins seldom visited by tourists are the types of activities that help make your trip unforgettable and truly unique. No matter how many suggestions you're given, regardless of how closely you follow this book, there will be countless chances on the road to discover and explore on your own. By using the information about advance planning and reading the "From Pounds to Pubs: A Taste of Everything Irish" section in this book, you will be well prepared to set out on Irish roads. Then let the tour descriptions be a general guide as you pedal, coast, and climb your way through one of the loveliest, friendliest places on earth.

ADVANCE PLANNING

THIS BOOK'S PERSPECTIVE. In order to put much of this book into some kind of perspective, it may help to understand my own views on cycling and traveling. I consider myself to be a moderate-ability cyclist who finds a 35- to 45-mile ride generally plenty for one day, although I can ride farther and have cycled a number of century (100-mile) rides. Because I prefer to see the sites rather than concentrate on mileage, I tend to average around 35 miles per day when cycling and noncycling days are counted together. That's why the tours in this book range in distances from 12 to 61 miles or so.

Of course, depending on your own abilities and opinions, the amount of time you have to spend, what you want to see, and to some extent, the weather, you may choose to combine tours, stop in the middle of tours, and certainly to vary from the described routes.

Another important thing to know about this book is that it is not intended to be a complete guide to accommodations and restaurants. Although I do note hostels, B&Bs, and campgrounds where they exist, I do not specifically endorse any or give prices. For that you should carry along information from the Irish Tourist Board (see Appendix 1) and/or travel guides such as *Frommer's* or *Ireland on US$50 a Day* (or whatever the dollar figure is now). Food is not something that is overly creative in Ireland, although it is quite sustaining, so it may be best to just strike out on your own in that regard and rely on chance and the locals for restaurant recommendations.

The routes in this book have been picked because along nearly all of them and at most of the destinations there are interesting sites, uncrowded roads, or gorgeous scenery. In some cases there is a combination of all three. Some routes take roundabout ways, others go in a more direct line. In each case, however, the direction picked was done so as to try to take advantage of the most scenery per mile, so to speak.

Finally, you should know that while the first edition of this book came about as a result of two fairly long tours of Ireland, this second edition results from my having personally toured with the first edition. More importantly, friends and family members have also used the book as a resource and contributed significantly to some important improvements and changes. Although things like opening hours of museums and names of commercial landmarks are not guaranteed to stay the same forever, the information in this book was accurate at the time it was written. Electronic mail and the Internet have enabled me to get current information even after I got back home.

WHEN TO GO. Ireland, as is the case with most destinations in the Northern Hemisphere, has its busiest time or "high season" during the summer. More specifically the months of July and August, and the first part of September, are the times it is likely to be the most crowded. August, in particular, is a busy month because of the number of other Europeans visiting Ireland at that time.

Not only does lodging get a little more difficult to come by during the high season, it also gets a little more expensive. For example, the price of many hostels goes up about a pound per night. For the majority of the year, calling and reserving a room at most hostels and B&Bs by the morning of the night you plan to stay is early enough. However, from late July through early September you may find it necessary to make reservations quite a bit sooner than that, especially in Dublin, Killarney, Dingle, Cork, and Galway.

On a cycling holiday, calling and reserving a week or two ahead of time can be a hassle and is sometimes an exercise in futility. It's hard to know exactly where you will be that many days in advance, and it doesn't leave room for much flexibility on the road. This is not to suggest that if you have to travel during the peak of the high season you won't find lodging. Calling a day or two ahead may still be sufficient to find a place, although you'll likely have to call around to two or three locations before finding a vacancy. Given that dilemma, try to travel from May through the first half of July if at all possible. That way you simply won't have the worry about not being able to find a room for the night. In addition, people traveling alone can almost always find a room in a hostel, and groups willing to split up can usually come up with something.

If you end up in Dublin during the high season without reservations, give serious consideration to staying in one of the suburbs. Not only do you escape the crowds, but you're much more likely to find lodging that suits you. As long as you are within walking distance of the train, this doesn't pose much hardship at all. In fact, I've stayed as far as an hour's train ride out, in Wicklow, and found it to be a very good tradeoff.

PASSPORTS. Well in advance of your departure, apply for a passport. Because of the potential of slow response times, allow *at least* a month for a new application to be processed. Renewals may take slightly less time. You can pick up passport forms at larger post offices, county courthouses, a federal, state, or probate court, or a regional passport agency. For more information about passports or to download a printable application visit the Bureau of Consular Affairs' passport information pages at http://travel.state.gov/passport_services.html.

Along with your application and fee of US$60, you must submit two photographs and a certified birth certificate. It's best to have the photos taken by a professional who specializes in passport photos. Snapshots are unacceptable. Passports are good for ten years, so you'll be able to go back to Ireland many times before you have to get a new one. Passport entry stamps are a good souvenir and reminder of your trip, but you may have to ask for the stamp as you pass through Irish customs. Many times the agents don't automatically do it. While traveling keep your passport in a safe, convenient location since it will be useful for activities such as exchanging money or renting bikes.

GETTING THERE. Airline prices to Ireland, just as to anywhere else, tend to fluctuate greatly from year to year and from season to season, so it's difficult to predict how much this expense will set you back. Undoubtedly though, this will be the largest single expense of the trip (unless, of course, you invest in a new titanium-frame bike). Prices generally range from US$650 to US$800 round trip, depending on departure date and destination. Flights in June through August tend to be considerably higher, so if you can travel in spring or fall you potentially stand to save a few hundred dollars. Be sure to inquire about charter flights. The flight may make more roundabout connections and take a little longer, but you can't grumble about the savings in price. If you decide to start your trip in Cork, Sligo, or Galway rather than from Dublin or Shannon you can get connections. Your flight will first land in either Dublin or Shannon and you'll transfer to a smaller craft for the domestic flight. See Part II of this book for more information on tours starting in Cork.

Your bicycle should, since this is an international flight, be counted as one of your checked bags for *no extra charge*, as long as your ticket says you're booked all the way to Ireland. For example, if you board in St. Louis, fly to New York, and then change planes, the flight from St. Louis to New York should be included as part of your international flight. Double-check this with your travel agent before buying your ticket. You may have to explain this policy at the domestic ticket counter when you arrive. For some reason, the clerks selling tickets and checking baggage seldom seem to know how to handle bikes going overseas. Weight and length of the box can sometimes be the deciding factor in whether the airline counts your bike as a piece of luggage or as extra baggage. Each airline has different regulations so, again, it's wise to check beforehand. Because of this, counting your bike as a piece of luggage gets a little trickier if you have an especially large bike such as a tandem. The section titled "Packing Your Bike" has more information on how to travel with your two-seater. Depending on how big they are, pannier bags can either be carried on or checked. If you do check them use strapping tape or heavy cord to hold them together so they don't get separated in transit. A handlebar pack makes a convenient carry-on and is a good place to keep track of passports, money, traveler's check receipts, and other difficult-to-replace items. A discussion about bringing your own bike versus renting one in Ireland follows in the next section.

RENTING VS. TRANSPORTING YOUR BIKE. In the first edition of this book I gave a strong recommendation that you should take your own bike on the trip and, in general, I still feel that way. On the other hand, the rental situation has improved through the years and there are decent reasons for leaving your bike at home and hiring one when you get there.

Since airlines don't charge extra for bikes on international flights it will be quite a lot cheaper just to take your own. That is, of course, unless you go out and buy a bike explicitly for the purpose of riding in Ireland. Second, you know what you're getting into in terms of quality when you've bought a bike at home and had lots of time to work out any bugs in it.

Third, with a rental you really can't be assured of a good fit. Think about how strange it feels to ride a friend's bike. Even if the fit is close, you still may not be entirely comfortable with it.

Ireland's many roadside shrines watch over faithful travelers.

On the other hand, it is possible nowadays to call ahead and reserve bikes in many of the larger or heavily touristed towns. You can request racks, toe clips, water bottles and cages, size, and the like. There are quite a few companies that rent bikes, so prices are rather reasonable. And some companies have shops in several towns, so if you need to have something fixed or exchange to a better fitting bike, service may be available en route.

Finally, hiring a bike saves you all the hassle of packing, worrying about whether your bike will be damaged or lost, and what to do with the box once you arrrive.

CHOOSING AND OUTFITTING A BIKE. When it comes to bikes, the cliché, "You get what you pay for," rings very true: Bikes from discount chains and mass merchandisers are typically made of cheap materials and are poorly assembled, heavy, and generally not fun to ride. In fact, I feel like I'm being fairly generous in that last sentence. If you're an avid cyclist you already know that, but if you're just getting into cycling you may wonder why there's such a price difference between bikes in the department stores and those in the bike shops. While it's not necessary for you to go out and buy a top-of-the-line bike, there are several factors you should keep in mind when deciding on a bike.

First, consider the type of travel you'll actually be doing. Most of your mileage will be on paved, although not always smooth, roads. So you'll want a bike with a sturdy frame.

Second, be sure to get a bike that fits you properly. The best way to do this is to shop local bike stores and find a salesperson who is knowledgeable about fit. No seat padding, gloves, or analgesic balm can make up for a bike that's the wrong size for you.

Third, you need a bike with plenty of gears. There will be numerous days of climbing in Ireland, and hauling twenty to thirty pounds of panniers uphill will make even seasoned cyclists reach for their easiest, or so-called granny, gears.

Fourth, make sure you buy a bike with moderately good components. Though not a complete list by any means, brands such as SunTour, Shimano, DuraAce, Campagnolo, and Mavic are all high-quality names. Shimano, in particular, puts its components on a wide range of bikes, including the previously discussed department store bikes, so name is not the only factor to consider.

With all of these criteria in mind, I believe the so-called hybrid or cross bike is the best type to use for touring in Ireland with a load of clothes and equipment. It has a fairly rigid frame, medium-width tires, and comfortable, upright fit. I have cycled on each of the three main types of bikes—road, mountain, and cross— and I am convinced that the hybrid is the one to take. This is not to say that road and mountain bikes won't work, but they do have their disadvantages.

Road bikes tend to have narrow tires, and in many places Irish roads can get pretty bumpy, causing a rough ride and more frequent flats. Always keep tires pumped to their maximum to prevent pinch flats from rough roads. In addition, the bent-back racing position is uncomfortable for many riders. Mountain bikes are probably second best, but because of the wide tires you'll tend to go slower on them. Although a bike with suspension is nice, it's not really necessary for on-road riding in Ireland.

If you already have a nice road or mountain bike, I'm not suggesting you go out and buy a different bike. In fact, I'd say save your money and spend it on a splurge in Ireland instead.

PACKING YOUR BIKE. There are three main ways of making sure your bike makes it to Ireland safely, and there is some disagreement among travelers as to which one is best. All of them have benefits and drawbacks, so you should decide for yourself which way sounds most likely to work. The first and simplest way to ship your bike is to slip it into one of the airline's plastic bike bags and have it sent aboard as is. Usually airlines require that you remove the pedals, turn the handlebars so they are parallel with the frame, and let some of the air out of the tires. This method takes very little time, but there is some risk in sending a virtually unprotected bike up the conveyor of a jumbo jet. Proponents of this idea believe that baggage handlers are less likely to damage a bike that's in plastic because things will not be stacked on it and it may be handled more gingerly. Pack some foam or bubble-wrap around the derailleurs as an added precaution; don't count on the baggage handlers to lay your bike down gently gear side up.

A second technique is to get a bike box from a bike shop and pack your bike in it. If you don't have experience breaking a bike down to fit in a box, let a bike mechanic do it for you. Watch it being done, though, and take note of what tools you'll need to pack so you can put your bike back together again. Be sure to remove especially sensitive parts such as computers and light systems. The bike should be well-padded, especially under and around the front fork and alongside the derailleurs. Padding won't guarantee the bike's protection, but if it's properly done, you'll know you did as much as you could reasonably do to get it there in one piece (so to speak). If there's room left over you can also store your helmet, bike shoes, and other larger items in the box. Don't overdo it though; you don't want to end up making your box too heavy. Use strapping or duct tape to go around your bike box numerous times. Make sure to wrap the tape around where the rear hub is poking up against the box. The tape might prevent it from working its way out.

A disadvantage of boxing your bike is having to decide what to do with the box once you have your bike back together and you're ready to pedal away. You have two main choices. First, you can just abandon the box at the airport and find a bike shop that can pack your bike for the flight home. If you take this route, arrange, a day in advance, for a taxi to take you and your bike to the airport for the return trip.

A second option is to have your bike taken, still boxed, to your first night's lodging. Put your bike together there, leave the box, and then stay there again on your last night in the country. Be sure to call ahead to see if this will be possible. Of course this alternative won't work if your departure city is not the same as your arrival city, in which case you'll have to ditch the box and start over.

The final, and costliest, way to ship your bike is in a specially made bike carrying case. These are available for around US$300 to US$400, and they provide superb protection. Realistically, nothing can absolutely guarantee that your bike won't get damaged, but if money is no object this is the way to go. Again, with this method you'll have to leave the case in a locker in the airport or at your first night's lodging. Check ahead to make sure either of these is possible.

If you're planning to take a tandem with you, a little more effort and planning is involved. I have shipped tandems in boxes and also in bags, both of which resulted in only minor scratches. I did lose a bag of pedals, however, through a hole in a box caused by rough handling. All of the tips in the preceding paragraphs apply to tandems. Even though your tandem is technically the baggage for two people, the airline won't count it that way so weight and overall size is very important.

To get around this problem, I recommend getting two boxes for each tandem. You'll have to take your bike apart considerably more for this, but doing so should help you get around the weight/size problem for the bike. The only time I've ever had to pay extra for my tandem is when I got an extremely large tandem box, one that I could fit the bike in without even taking off the tires.

WHAT TO BRING. What follows is a discussion of the items you should consider taking along on a cycling trip to Ireland. Although part of the fun is deciding what to take and what to leave behind, these are some of the items I've found—occasionally because I didn't have them—to be extremely valuable. It's also worth noting that if you do forget something you really need, you can probably buy it in Ireland. It's a fairly rural country, but it's not a wilderness.

The key to this trip, as to any other, is found in the adage "travel light." You'll no doubt collect souvenirs along the way, so leave empty space accordingly.

Cash for Starting Out. I urge you to convert US$100 to US$200 (depending on your spending habits) into Irish currency before you leave home. Large banks may carry Irish pounds, and even small banks can send the money off to be exchanged. The exchange rate may not be quite as good, but when you arrive wrestling with jet lag's effects, you'll be glad you don't need to go in search of an exchange office or a bank. Besides, it's fun to carry the money in your wallet or purse and show it off to your friends.

Most people buy travelers checks before going overseas, and I would like to reinforce this idea when you go to Ireland. Not only are they safer than cash, but you get a better exchange rate. Because of the rate, the best place to exchange travelers checks is at a bank. That said, it may also be a good idea to use your credit card for as many purchases as possible. VISA, MasterCard, and

Eurocard are all widely accepted. When you charge items you will almost always get a much better exchange than you would by exchanging for cash. Before you go, however, call your credit card company and find out what the percentage rate is for foreign currency transactions. It shouldn't be much over one percent. If it is, consider getting a different card. The main disadvantage of relying on credit cards is that some B&Bs and hostels won't accept them.

With the growth of electronic financial networks it is rather easy to use your ATM card to get cash in most locales. Because most ATM transactions are charged a flat fee and not a percentage, if you make a few large withdrawals you'll still lose less in charges than you would by exchanging traveler's checks. ATMs can be found at many banks and most will accept credit cards, particularly VISA and MasterCard, as well as the Plus and Cirrus debit cards.

While traveling with plastic is very convenient, there are a few things you should keep in mind about being too reliant on it. First, it's a good idea to have at least some cash on hand at all times. Smaller towns may not have cash machines or it may not be an opportune moment for you to get to them. Second, because cards can get lost, be stolen, or have the magnetic coding corrupted, it's a good idea to carry at least two cards.

Rain Gear. High-quality rain gear is essential since it will likely rain several times during your trip. Don't skimp when it comes to keeping yourself dry. If you're experienced at riding in a steady rain, you already realize how important this is. If not, try standing in a mild rain for three or four hours and then keeping the same clothes on the rest of the day. Got the picture? It's a little disheartening to have to hop on a bike in the morning in a pouring rain, but good rain gear provides some comfort.

Many touring bikes come equipped with fenders. If yours doesn't, it's not a bad idea to get at least a rear fender. Though no one will confuse you for a racer in the *Tour de France*, a fender prevents you from getting a wet, muddy back and will minimize trips to the laundry.

Packs. The types and number of packs you carry depends on the sort of trip you're planning. If you intend to camp, you'll likely need the full complement of front and rear panniers plus a handlebar bag to haul all your gear. If you'll be staying in bed and breakfasts or hostels, the front or rear panniers and a handlebar pack should be sufficient.

When it comes to packs, there is a variety of styles and brands from which to choose. Whichever kind you choose, be sure it is lightweight, durable, unlikely to rip or tear, and at least somewhat rain resistant. For really dry gear, store items in watertight plastic bags. This also can help you locate needed items without digging everything out of your pack. Rainproof pack covers are especially useful, not only in keeping packs dry but also clean. They come in bright colors which will help make you more visible on rainy days. Because your handlebar pack will likely hold your map, passport, money, and other important papers, it is especially important that it be rainproof.

Tools and Parts. If you plan to be a more or less self-sufficient rider, a good supply of tools is imperative. The following should be in your tool pack:

- wrenches for brakes, cable anchors, pedals and wheels (if you don't have quick release)
- cable cutters
- extra brake and derailleur cables
- chain oil
- extra tubes and/or patch kit
- spare, foldable tire
- tire levers
- small screwdrivers to fit your bike
- tire pump that attaches to frame
- Allen wrenches for handlebars and seat posts
- spoke wrench and three or four extra spokes
- rag for cleaning off grease
- duct tape (I know that's not a standard piece of bike equipment but it is extremely useful in a pinch)
- bike lock and key

Being self-sufficient is a good goal but there will probably be times when you need repairs that you can't make on the road. Fortunately, bike shops are common in Ireland and are usually well equipped. In fact, it's almost unbelievable how easy it is to get parts and service even in small towns. Because so many more Europeans ride bikes than do Americans, there is a much better repair infrastructure in Ireland. Even if there's no bike shop per se, you can check at petrol stations, hardware stores, or other similar establishments. Someone is bound to be able to either fix your bike or give you the name of someone who can.

For example, on my most recent tour of Ireland I was with eight other cyclists. About 2 miles from Kilrush on a Saturday afternoon, one of my companions, who had been riding on an out-of-true rear wheel, had several spokes break. While the rest of us went on into town to find our hostel and to try to locate a bike shop, he and his wife walked the bike the rest of the way. By the time he got to town we had located a hardware store that also did bike repairs. Unfortunately it was past 5:00 P.M. and the repairman was gone for the day. In fact, the shop was preparing to close up.

We had planned to leave Kilrush the next morning but now realized that we would end up staying until Monday, when the shop opened again. However, as we stood there pondering our dilemma and trying to figure out how we could somehow rig the bike, the shop's owner happened in. After he finished answering a customer's questions about some fishing equipment, the clerk relayed our story to the owner. Glancing only momentarily at his watch, the owner told us to bring the bike around the corner where his equipment was. Within an hour the wheel was good as new and we were once again ready to ride. The total charge for this custom, emergency service was around US$25.

Clothing. Everyone has his or her own preferences when it comes to clothes, but a few guidelines or suggestions may help you slim down the possibilities. Ireland is a casual country, and there is really no need to pack anything fancy. The same sweater you wear on cold, rainy rides will work for going out to dinner. If you end up needing something nice, buy it in Ireland and call it a souvenir. Stick with clothes that don't wrinkle easily, since being stuffed into a pack tends to crumple everything. Lycra clothing fits this criterion well, and if you don't feel uncomfortable or conspicuous wearing skin-tight shorts in public they work great. Others may wish to carry along some larger, baggier shorts to slip on when they get to their destination.

Jeans or some other type of long pants are great to have along and may feel rather luxurious after several days of wearing nothing but riding shorts. And since the nights are chilly, you really will need something other than shorts on your legs. Don't take cotton t-shirts or sweatshirts. You'll probably handwash clothes frequently, and synthetic materials or synthetic/cotton blends tend to dry faster.

Bring along at least one other pair of shoes besides your riding shoes. Since you'll most likely be riding in the rain a lot, you won't want to tour castles and go to dinner in sodden shoes. Ankle-length, rather than calf-length, socks are better since recurrent rains can make drying socks a frequent pastime.

If you're cycling in summer, Ireland's temperatures are relatively mild during the day but considerably cooler at night. A sweater or medium-weight jacket will keep you toasty on some of those chilly evenings on the coast. Better than bringing one from home is buying an Aran wool sweater when you get there.

I strongly encourage you to wear a hard-shell helmet whenever you ride. A bit uncomfortable but something you can get used to, a helmet is now looked on as a prerequisite to safe riding by most touring cyclists. Besides, a head injury is a quick way to end a vacation (or a life). Don't let it bother you that you may be one of the few people wearing a helmet since, according to one native, Americans are the only ones wearing them. Padded gloves also make for more comfortable riding and help prevent fatigue in hand and wrist muscles.

The central idea, again, is to travel light and carry as few clothes as you can. Bring items that are suitable for both riding and walking; you'll certainly be stopping quite often, and changing clothes is an unnecessary hassle.

PACKING YOUR GEAR. Loading up and assembling your supplies is not only one of your last steps before departure, it's also one of the most important. To begin, the handlebar pack serves very well as a camera bag and daypack, especially if it comes with a carrying strap. The pack should slip on and off the bike easily so the camera is always close at hand. This way, you may even be able to get to the camera while riding. Sheep scuffling down a backcountry road or a passing flock of gulls may not wait for you to dig out a buried camera.

A well-kept thatched cottage gives this cycling pair a taste of "traditional" Ireland.

Put important papers such as return plane tickets, passports, and money in the handlebar pack so they are never far out of reach (or sight). A saddlebag can serve the same purpose, but is not as easy to get into in a hurry. For less comfort but greater security, you can always try a money belt or some other kind of wallet that you can put around your neck or shoulder and wear inside your clothes.

To balance your belongings and make for a smoother ride, the remainder of your gear should be evenly distributed in your panniers. Make sure to pack in a logical sequence. Things you will use often, such as toiletries, tools, and your guidebook, ought to be placed on top or toward the outside. Souvenirs and extra shoes fit best on the bottom-inside of a pack. When you're not wearing your rainsuit, keep it readily available.

PRETRIP PLANNING MATERIALS. Another step in your pretrip preparation is to arm yourself with a cache of practical information and advice. The Irish Tourist Board, *Bord Failte* (pronounced *board folchu*), is one of the finest of its kind in the world. It publishes pamphlets and brochures on subjects ranging from where to stay and what to do, to county guides and restaurant menus.

You can pick up a wealth of free or inexpensive materials at the tourist office (or *"i,"* which means information) in most large cities or in heavily visited locations during the peak season. Where you see the green *"i"* or the sign *"Oifig Failte"* (Welcome Office) you'll find an abundance of materials to assist you.

The Irish Tourist Board has its headquarters in Dublin, but in the United States write to 345 Park Avenue, New York, NY 10154 or call 212/418-0800. The Tourist Board also has a website located at http://www.ireland.travel.ie/home/index.asp. The information you receive from them will be invaluable in your planning. Some of the Irish Tourist Board's excellent publications are listed in Appendix 1. Inquire about other topics if you don't find what you're looking for in this list. In addition, Appendix 1 also lists a number of potentially useful websites for locating information about Ireland.

Maps. Of all the material you will find useful, no doubt your most constant companion will be your road map. Once again, the Tourist Board can provide many. Some are very detailed, and others are of no practical use to cyclists. Michelin's Map No. 405 covers all of the Republic of Ireland and Northern Ireland and has consistent numbering with both the old and new numbering systems used on Irish roads. (See "From Pounds to Pubs" for more information on roads.) This, plus the route maps in this book, should be adequate to get you where you are trying to go. For really getting off the "beaten path" and onto roads that are not marked on the Michelin series map, try the Ordnance Survey maps available at most tourist offices.

All distances in this book are given in miles, both in the text and on the maps, as distances on road signs are generally given in miles. Occasionally, signs will have both miles and kilometers on them and, rarely, will have only kilometers. If you find a sign in kilometers only, simply multiply the number by 0.7 to convert the number to miles. For example, 10 kilometers equals 7 miles (10 kilometers x 0.7 = 7 miles).

Many cyclists find a small compass useful when riding on many of the narrow, twisting country lanes. Since the sun is frequently not visible, it is rather easy to lose your sense of direction, and with a compass you can orient the map better at crossroads and other decision points.

This section has focused on the kinds of preparations you need to make while still in your home country. By taking some time and expending a little effort, your trip to Ireland, perhaps a once-in-a-lifetime experience, will be well on its way to being more carefree and memorable. Although your plans will certainly change along the way, by reading the tourist booklets, packing the right clothes, and seeing that your bike is safely transported, you will have better knowledge and more freedom to make the frequent "left fork–right fork" decisions that will certainly come your way.

The Fine Print. Although I have made every attempt to make sure the information contained in this book is accurate, changes will inevitably occur. At times, throughout the book, certain signs or buildings are used as reference points to give distances or directions on when to turn. As is the case anywhere in the world, signs are changed, hotels go out of business or change their names, and even more dramatically, roads are rerouted. As time marches on, progress may even make a narrow two-lane road into a busy dual carriageway. Whenever these things happen and you are unsure of the correct route to take, it is generally a good idea simply to stop and ask someone for directions. Fortunately, you are cycling through a very friendly, helpful country. I welcome any comments you may have regarding such changes and heartily encourage them.

No attempt is made in this book to recommend restaurants, lodgings, or other commercial tourist services. What may be an excellent hostel in my view may not be one in yours, thus any remarks about specific establishments is implicitly not to be viewed as a recommendation to patronize it.

FROM POUNDS TO PUBS:
A TASTE OF EVERYTHING IRISH

CURRENCY AND EXCHANGE. Irish currency is officially known as "the Punt," or "the Irish Pound" but you'll seldom hear anyone call it that. No matter how nationalistic, the Irish nearly always just call it "the pound."

The pound is divided into 100 pence. Commonly used denominations of coins include the 1 pence (1p), 2p, 5p, 10p, 20p, 50p, and 1 pound (£1). Notes or bills regularly used are the 5, 10, and 20. It's better, though it takes up more room, to carry mostly small bills and several 1-pound coins. Smaller businesses may have difficulty making change for larger denominations.

The rate of exchange varies daily. On a day when £1=US$1.65, an item costing £10 would cost US$16.50. In the past few years the rate has been up to a high of US$1.85 to US$1.90, but it fluctuates quite frequently. Keep an eye on the business section of the newspaper for up-to-date quotes. Don't expect to get the same rate, though, since those quotes are for multimillion dollar exchanges. However, they can serve as a rough guide to the rates. Appendix 2 will help you convert pounds to dollars for several exchange rates and will let you know how much you're actually spending for your purchases.

Three common banks are the Allied Irish Bank, Bank of Ireland, and the Ulster Bank, where you'll almost always find a special window for foreign exchange transactions. This means you won't have to wait while customers deposit money, pay mortgages, and the like, and you'll usually be out of the bank in under ten minutes. When exchanging traveler's checks you'll have to show your passport. Also keep in mind not to sign the checks until you're in the presence of the clerk.

Hotels, shops, and airports usually charge higher fees for exchanging currency, and/or the exchange rate may be lower by several percent. The common name for the exchange office in Ireland, as in the rest of Europe, is French: Bureau de Change.

Appendix 3 lists a variety of items you will likely spend money on and their 1998 prices. Though prices will almost certainly be higher by the time you travel, these can at least act as a relative guide for the expense of a few common items.

LANGUAGE AND LITERATURE. English and Irish (or Gaelic as it's also called) are the two national languages of Ireland, but in practice very few people speak Gaelic. Though over the past few years it has been enjoying a revival, only in small parts of the west does Gaelic thrive. Quite a lot of Irish is spoken in places such as the Aran Islands or in the Connemara region northwest of Galway. These places are known as *Gaeltachts,* and Gaelic is officially promoted in these areas. According to the Tourist Bureau, about thirty percent of the adult population of Ireland claim some knowledge of the language. Generally even those who speak Gaelic will slip into English to give you directions or to converse about the damp weather. I doubt you'll ever meet anyone who simply won't or can't speak English. Even the English, though, has a bewitching lilt that you'll probably imitate unconsciously for weeks after you return home.

Nearly all the road signs employ both languages. For example, the sign indicating 14 miles to Kilgarvan includes the Irish *"Cill Gharbhain"* above it. Because English is almost always there, you shouldn't have any trouble figuring out where you are or where you're supposed to turn.

The Gaelic pronunciation of words is considerably different from that of English. In fact, for those of us whose experience with foreign languages is limited to maybe a little high school Spanish or French, the pronunciation is so challenging that you'll probably not find a lot of opportunities to speak Gaelic. Still, I suggest that you pick up a simple Irish phrase book. While it's not prerequisite to fruitful sightseeing, you may be able to translate a few words from road signs, billboards, and Gaelic-language newspapers.

To get yourself into an Irish frame of mind while you're counting down the days to the start of your trip, read up on Irish history and explore the writings Ireland has inspired. I can almost guarantee that if you don't do at least some homework before you go, you'll regret it when you get there. After my first trip I came home and devoured everything about Ireland I could get my hands on because I was so unprepared when I went. What follows is a list of novels and chronicles that I recommend.

- *Ireland: A Terrible Beauty* by Jill and Leon Uris. An easy-to-read history of Ireland with an excellent explanation of the mid- to late-twentieth-century problems between the Republic of Ireland and Northern Ireland.
- *Trinity* by Leon Uris. A riveting, historically based novel about the plight of the Irish "croppy" and his struggle to throw off the oppressive chains of British rule.
- *The Collected Poems of W. B. Yeats.* As the title suggests, this is an assembly of a number of Yeats's more famous works. If you're planning to tour the northwest, particularly around Sligo, then this is a must-read since that is considered Yeats's country.
- *The Tain,* translated by Thomas Kinsella. A look at eighth-century (and

earlier) Irish literature that describes, very elegantly, the attempted theft of a prize bull and the rise of the Irish hero Cuchulainn.

- *The Islandman* by Tomas O'Crohan. An authentic look at life on the nearly deserted Blasket Islands by a man who lived out his life there. Covers the period from the mid-1850s to the early 1930s.
- *Twenty Years A-Growing* by Maurice O'Sullivan. Stories covering the early to mid-twentieth century on the Blaskets. Mentions some of the same characters as O'Crohan's book except they are seen as older men rather than peers.
- *An Old Woman's Reflections* by Peig Sayers. By another author who grew up on the Blasket Islands, this book fits well with the books by O'Crohan and O'Sullivan. Sayers writes from the perspective of an elderly woman about the days of her youth on the Blaskets.
- *Ulysses* by James Joyce. Hats off to you if you can wade through this now classic story that follows the parallel lives of Leopold Bloom and Stephen Dedalus in early-twentieth-century Dublin. Difficult reading but worth it to get an idea of the classic flavor of Dublin. English teachers and ravenous readers aside, for a realistic chance at understanding more than half the book, consider getting the Cliffs Notes and alternate between reading them and the book. By the way, Dedalus is also the subject of an earlier work by Joyce, *A Portrait of the Artist as a Young Man.*
- *Dubliners* by James Joyce. This collection of short stories details the lives of several "average" citizens of Dublin. All in all, kind of a depressing book but much easier reading than some of Joyce's other works.
- *A Treasury of Irish Folklore*, edited by Padraic Colum. Collection of stories and fireside tales about ancient heroes, former leaders, and old ways and traditions. Includes several pages of ballads and songs with their accompanying tunes.
- *Irish Myth, Legend, and Folklore.* A combined volume of folk tales edited by W.B. Yeats with a recounting of many stories about Cuchulainn by Lady Isabella Augusta Gregory.

TELEPHONE SERVICE. The first thing to keep in mind about phoning from the United States to Ireland is that Ireland is five hours ahead of Eastern Standard Time. To make a call to anywhere in Ireland from the United States, dial 011 353 (011 is an international access code, and 353 is the specific country code for Ireland), then dial the number of the Irish locale.

For example, let's say you are trying to call the Dingle Tourist Office. You would dial 011 353 66 51188. The 66 is Dingle's telephone prefix, and 51188 is the number for the *Bord Failte* office in Dingle.

When you're calling within Ireland to a different telephone prefix, add a 0 to the prefix. For example, if you're calling from outside Dingle to the number used in the example above, dial 066 51188. When you're calling to and from the same telephone prefix, dial only the number and leave the prefix off altogether. For example, if you're calling from one Killarney bed and breakfast to another, dial 32184 instead of 064 32184. Use the prefix only when calling to a different prefix, such as Killarney (064) to Dingle (066).

Currently there are two types of public phones in Ireland. One is the traditional coin phone, which requires a minimum of 20p for most calls. Many of the newer phones of this type have a display showing how much of your deposit remains. This helps you judge how much time you have left on the call. The other type of public phone is the "CALLCARD" phone, which will not accept coins. Instead you must insert a special plastic card that can be purchased in a number of shops and some post offices. The microchip on the front of the card tells the phone how much your card is worth. You never waste change with these cards since the phone subtracts just the amount the call costs. However, if your card becomes fully depleted while you are talking on the phone, your call will be cut off, unless you are prepared with a fresh, unused card to insert into the slot.

Calling home to the United States from Ireland has been made much simpler over the years with the proliferation of international access calling cards. With some of these cards, all you do is dial an 800 number and you will be connected to an operator in the United States. You then give the operator your billing information.

TAX REFUNDS. Residents of non-European Economic Community countries such as the United States are entitled to Value Added Tax (VAT) credits on many purchases made in Ireland. Since the amount of the tax varies from ten to twenty percent, this can amount to a considerable sum of money. In order to receive a refund, you must fill out a CASHBACK voucher where you make your purchase. Most shops have a sticker indicating that they participate in the program. If a shop doesn't have the sticker, ask before making the purchase. You must have the voucher to get a refund.

When leaving the country, take the voucher to the CASHBACK counter in either Shannon or Dublin airport. You'll receive your money back in dollars or pounds, depending on which you prefer, less a service charge. There is a charge for each separate voucher, so you'll save money by buying several items in one shop rather than a number of shops.

THE LAND AND ITS PEOPLE. The Republic of Ireland contains just over 27,000 square miles, making it about the same size as West Virginia. But because of all the nooks and crannies etched into its shore, it has over a thousand miles of coastline.

Ireland consists of thirty-two counties, which are gathered into four provinces. The provinces and their counties are:

ULSTER: Cavan, Donegal, Monaghan, all in the Republic of Ireland, and Antrim, Armagh, Derry, Down, Fermanagh, and Tyrone all in Northern Ireland.

Note: Many associate Ulster specifically with Northern Ireland but as you can see from this list, that is not technically correct.

LEINSTER: Carlow, Dublin, Kildare, Kilkenny, Laois, Longford, Louth, Meath, Offaly, Westmeath, Wexford, and Wicklow.

MUNSTER: Clare, Cork, Kerry, Limerick, Tipperary, and Waterford.

CONNAUGHT: Sligo, Mayo, Galway, Roscommon, and Leitrim.

The majority of the land is used as meadow or pasture. In fact, less than twenty percent is arable, and only about five percent is forested. While to some the Irish landscape may look rather desolate, most of the land is in some kind of agricultural production. Irish farmers make up almost ten percent of the work force and are responsible for a large agricultural trade surplus. Ireland's strong agricultural base makes the country fairly self-sufficient in food, lacking only in bread grain and a few fruits and vegetables. Indeed, there are nearly three times as many sheep and twice as many cattle as there are people in this relatively small country. Besides the tremendous quantity of farm products, the land also provides thousands of tons of fertilizers, cement, iron, steel, and coal.

Rolling hills and lush, verdant countryside dominate Ireland's prominent coastal areas; however, variations in topography abound. Long, largely flat stretches are interspersed with strenuous grades ascending into low-flying clouds. In the west, many of the roads take you right along the coast with spectacular views of precipitous sea cliffs, like those that trace the Ring of Kerry or outline the Dingle Peninsula. Farther inland is the Burren, a somber landscape under-laid with massive slabs of limestone and dotted with wildflowers.

The middle of the country comprises the flatter, somewhat less dramatic regions, much as the Plains states do in the United States. This does provide excellent riding terrain, but you may have to travel farther between interesting towns and attractions. On the other hand, the ruins at Kells, and the towns of Cashel and Kilkenny are sites that really should not be missed.

Whereas the mountains of the west are principally composed of sedimentary rock from ancient seas, the Wicklow Mountains in the east deliver a rocky contrast. Granite and other types of volcanic rock formations govern the landscape and reflect a fiery formation. This type of terrain provided excellent protection from invasion for such places as Glendalough, which features monastic ruins from the Middle Ages tucked amid the crags and peaks.

In the northwest and the Connemara region, mountains lie between spongy bogs rich in peat and innumerable sheep. At times the road will wander for miles with no sign of civilization save the asphalt under your tires, ever-present electrical lines, and the occasional passing car.

As of the 1996 census Ireland had over 3.6 million people, the greatest population number since 1881. Dublin is by far the largest city, with around a million people, followed by Cork with 180,000 and Limerick with 79,000. Galway and Waterford round out the top five cities in terms of population.

Overgrown stone bridges such as this one carry much of Ireland's rural traffic.

Nearly seventy percent of Ireland's population is under the age of forty-five, and over twenty percent is under fifteen. This bodes well for Ireland's future population growth, as well as its ability to maintain its economic growth and labor force well into the twenty-first century.

WEATHER. The only thing predictable about Irish weather is that it will almost definitely rain on you during some part of your trip. Tours of the west seem especially damp. Actually, they don't just seem that way, on average they are. Whereas Dublin, on the east, receives about 80 centimeters of rain per year, County Kerry gets around 150 centimeters. However, the misery of a soggy cyclist doesn't go unnoticed by the natives. In the spirit of typical Irish hospitality, the proprietress of one Galway bed and breakfast exclaimed sincerely that she was "quite sick of the rain" herself, and she wondered if I wouldn't come to her dining room to dry off with a steamy cup of tea and a large piece of rhubarb pie. In fact, you might find that the Irish, in general, have an overall apologetic attitude about the weather. This is not to say that a tour of Ireland by bicycle will be unpleasant.

Storms are ordinarily rather mild, and severe ones are infrequent. Though Ireland lies at about the same latitude as Edmonton, Canada, the North Atlantic current has a moderating effect on the climate. It seldom gets too hot or too cold. In fact, most days, rainy or not, are remarkably pleasant. However, on cloudy days, even in the summer, the wind can be rather chilly and you may find yourself wearing long sleeves or your rain jacket just to take the edge off the wind. When the sun does shine, the air is crisp and clean (unless you're in Dublin or Cork), and your skin is liable to burn in a hurry without sunblock. Nights are very chilly, especially along the coast.

Whenever you can, cover your longer trips on dry days, then hole up and explore the local area when the weather turns too dreary. Rain usually starts as a slight drizzle and continues until you're completely soaked. Then follows brilliant sun and uncommonly blue skies. Two hours later you may be slipping your rain gear back on and cursing your decision to come to this rainy place. You'll probably get used to the frequent showers, and even if you don't, you can always pull into a roadside pub and chat with the locals. A round of Guinness and the chummy atmosphere will make the rain and soppy bike gloves seem inconsequential.

TRAFFIC AND ROAD CONDITIONS. Though the weather is often a hard pill to swallow, the roads are genuinely a spoonful of sugar, even though it is true that because of the frequent showers the roads are often "slippy." Although the main highway around Dublin has been compared to a "middle-aged U.S. Interstate" and some reports declare the roads "twist like an Irish tale," Irish roads are generally in decent shape. Keep in mind that this is a rural country; only around the big cities will you find four-lane highways ("dual carriageways"). That means most of your riding will be on somewhat narrow, two-lane roads. Actual road surface conditions vary, just as they do in the United States, but most roads are negotiable with a typical touring, hybrid, or mountain bike.

The Irish drive on the left side of the road. This is not difficult to get used to, but it requires some adjustment. For example, a left turn is the easy one to make, and you may need to move your rearview mirror to the other side of your bike.

Irish road markings have changed throughout the years, and many maps still contain both the old and new markings. Essentially, four letters are used to name the various roads. The larger, more direct routes are labeled as N (National Primary Route) or T (Trunk, the old name). For example, the route from Ennis to Kilrush is N68 or T41. Secondary routes begin with either R (Regional) or L (Link). The road from Lahinch to Doolin is called both R478 and L54. In this book, I include both numbers for each road when available and appropriate. In addition, a new type of road, the M, or Motorway, has sprung up around Dublin. **Bicycles, as well as other slow-moving vehicles and pedestrians, are excluded from using these roads.**

One nice thing about Irish roads is that you don't have to take a longer, oblique route in order to "see the countryside." Many of the primary routes are marked "scenic"; there are very few roads I have traveled that don't have at least some nice scenery to make the trip pleasant, whether marked that way or not.

The best aspect of the road conditions in Ireland is the motorists who use them. Not once in thousands of miles of cycling have I heard an intolerant horn or received an obscene gesture. You understand the importance of this when you're riding around blind curves, inches from a stone fence with two or three cars trailing you. Irish drivers are blessed with the virtue of patience, and many wave a courteous hello as they pass you by. The only time you may feel a bit cramped is on the busier roads in heavily touristed areas. The buses often do not give you much room and infrequently you may be forced so close to the edge that you have to stop. This is a rare occurrence but bear it in mind when you see that bus coming in your mirror. Tour numbers 8 and 9 around the Ring of Kerry and the daytrip around Slea Head in Tour 10 are particularly full of tour buses.

Ireland's highway department must have a special bureau for creating unusual road signs. Though most can be attributed to slight differences between Irish English and American English, the signs themselves are worth watching for. Loose gravel, for example, becomes "loose chippings," and to warn against flying debris the sign says "protect your windscreen." Dangerous curves are "acute bends," detours are "diversions," and slippery roads are "slippy." Even better are the wordless signs such as the one in a parking lot indicating the harbor dead ahead. It simply shows a car plunging off the pier into the water. That one is an attention grabber.

ACCOMMODATIONS. There are many choices to make about where to stay while you're in Ireland. In this book, I provide information on the four options best suited to a cyclist on a low to average budget: bed and breakfasts (B&Bs), hostels, self-catering homes, and campgrounds. Appendix 1 lists the Irish Tourist Board publications that describe the availability of these around the country.

In the first edition of this book I strongly recommended B&Bs as the best lodging value in Ireland. After my most recent return I now rank them as my second choice. Because the number of hostels has increased significantly in the past few years, and their service and quality has generally improved as well, hostels are now my personal preference. In addition, they are considerably less expensive than B&Bs. Still, no matter which lodging option you choose, you will almost always find friendly people who will do what they can to make your stay a good one.

Bed and Breakfasts. B&Bs are by far the most widespread of all the lodging options. It seems that nearly every road you travel, even in fairly remote areas, will offer several. And any time you come to a village or town, you will undoubtedly come across at least one. Even the countryside is dotted with myriad farmhouses that serve as B&Bs.

Many B&Bs are listed and approved by the Irish Tourist Board (ITB) and display the "Approved" sign flanked by two shamrocks. Though I suppose it's possible to find an approved B&B that isn't worthwhile, it's very unlikely, and the approval sign is a good indication of cleanliness and adherence to standards. If you ever have any reason for complaint, *Bord Failte* recommends that you try to settle it with the owner first. If you're not satisfied then contact the nearest *Bord Failte* office.

Some of these approved B&Bs are also members of the Town & Country Homes association, which publishes a booklet (see Appendix 1) with pictures of the homes and thorough descriptions of services. If you're planning to stay in

B&Bs, this is a good booklet to have and is much smaller than the complete listing of ITB-approved residences. In addition, you will often come across B&Bs that are not listed by either ITB or Town & Country Homes. Most of these are probably okay as well. The disadvantages are that you don't know the price beforehand and there is no way to phone ahead for reservations. The Town & Country Homes website is found at http://www.commerce.ie/towns_and_country/. This useful site has a searchable directory of member B&Bs to help you locate one.

There are many wonderful characteristics about B&Bs that make them great places to stay. Depending on the current exchange rate, B&Bs average between US$23 and US$28 (£15 and £18) per night. For this price you get friendly conversation, tea, a cozy bed, a hearty breakfast, and various other pleasant surprises. Please note that because very few B&Bs have single rooms, a solo traveler usually must pay a supplement. Though this may range from £3 to £7 in addition to the per-person price, B&Bs are still a reasonably good value. B&Bs generally charge £1 to £2 more for a private bath as well. If you want this option ask for a room "en suite." If you don't mind sharing a hallway bath and toilet, ask for a normal or regular room. Also of importance: A "double" is a room with one double bed; a "twin" is a room with two single beds.

Breakfast usually consists of orange juice, toast, real butter, brown bread, marmalade and jam, cereal, and a bottomless pot of tea or coffee. And this is only for starters. Then comes bacon (called rashers) and/or sausage, eggs, toast, and perhaps a grilled tomato. (*Note:* If you are offered black pudding, it is fried blood sausage. White pudding is more like what Americans call sausage.) For most people, this is more than enough for several hours and it makes a good fuel supply (though a little fatty) for a day of riding. The breakfast, if bought in a restaurant, would cost at least US$6 to US$8 (£4 to £7), so if you're a big breakfast eater you should factor that in when considering the value of the B&B.

A few other features B&Bs have over camping are protection from the rain and elements, close proximity to local attractions, and the security of having a place to leave your bike and gear while you're out eating, visiting museums, or lounging in a pub. Many will fix dinner for you if you like. (Ordinarily you must request this before noon. The price is usually about the same as for bed and breakfast so it's rather expensive. For example, if your bed is costing you £15 so will your dinner.) There's also something nice about having a hot shower, a soft mattress, and a quiet room that makes the rigors of the road easier to take.

Over the past several years the number of B&Bs seems to have increased significantly. There are a number of facilities that have been built expressly as B&Bs. I suppose the increased competition helps keep the price down, but I also believe that many of the newer, larger establishments have taken away a bit of the original charm of the B&B. Many of the six- to ten-room places feel more like hotels than someone's home and are a lot less personal. My favorite B&Bs

are usually rather small, with only a few bedrooms that have become available as sons or daughters have left the nest. The people who run these tend to be quick to offer tea and snacks when you arrive, to light a fire on a chilly night, to serve marvelously filling breakfasts, and to share their opinions on things to see and routes to take. Often these more personal residences are outside of town a mile or two or are in smaller towns. Still, personal or not, B&Bs typically provide adequate amenities and do well at what their name suggests.

Hostels. There are three main types of hostels in Ireland. One type is those that are members of the Irish Youth Hostel Association (IYH), *An Oige.* Currently there are thirty-seven IYH hostels throughout the Republic of Ireland. As is the case with any IYH-affiliated hostel, you must have a membership card in order to stay there. In all of the hostels, it is recommended that you bring a sheet bag, although these can usually be rented for a small fee at the hostel. (A sheet bag can be made by sewing two twin sheets together so the bag can slip over a mattress or so you can slip in the bag.) IYH prices range from about £6.50 to £9.50. For more information contact *An Oige* at 61 Mountjoy Street, Dublin 7 (phone 01 8304555) or e-mail at anoige@iol.ie. You can also visit their website at http://www.commerce.ie/anoige.

Other hostels are members of the Independent Holiday Hostel Association (IHH). The hostels in this organization have grown to be my personal favorite. All of these IHH hostels are inspected and approved by the Irish Tourist Board or the Northern Ireland Tourist Board and require no membership. The hostels cater to all ages, and many have family rooms available. The official listing of IHH hostels is called The Guinness Guide and it can be obtained by writing to the ITB (see Appendix 1). Information about the hostels and a list with addresses and phone numbers is on their website at http://www.iol.ie/hostel.

There are 150 IHH hostels so nearly all of Ireland's counties are covered. With a few exceptions the hostels are clean, relatively quiet, and have friendly staff. They don't have curfews, and in cases where the doors are locked at night, you are either given a key or a security code to work the door. Many of these hostels occupy restored buildings near the town center so they make a very convenient base from which to tour. Though they don't all have a storage shed or garage for bikes, they will all find a way to make your bike secure. In two or three of these hostels we simply brought our bikes in and were able to lock them up in the hostel's hallways.

Though IHH hostels are usually a little more expensive (£8–£12 per person) than *An Oige* hostels they make up for it in lack of curfew, their proximity to towns and attractions, and the fact that they are more widespread. You can plan your route around the entire country and be able to stay in an IHH hostel almost each night. If you plan to do this you can take advantage of their Book Ahead System. The hostel staff will call your next hostel for you and for £6 will give you a ticket guaranteeing you a bed. Then you pay the balance due once you get there. You can contact the IHH by e-mail at ihh@iol.ie or write to them at IHH Office, 57 Lower Gardiner St., Dublin 1, Ireland (phone 01 836 4700).

Still a third type of hostel is those that are members of the Independent Hostel Owners Association. There are about the same number of hostels in this organization as in IHH. The Independent Owners can be contacted at: Information Office, Dooey Hostel, Glencolmcille, Co Donegal, Ireland (phone 073 30130). Their website address is http://www.epcmedia.net/ihi/.

Self-Catering Homes. Besides touring on a loaded bike, there is another option for bicycle travel in Ireland. Many locations throughout the country offer what the Irish call self-catering homes. These are cottages, farmhouses, apartments, and, in some cases, even castles that are available for lease on a weekly basis. The homes provide cooking and cleaning facilities, food storage space, a place to sleep, and bathing/toilet facilities at the very minimum. Other services, which vary by location, include television, dishwasher, washing machine, and babysitting. A guide to self-catered accommodations can be purchased from the Irish Tourist Board. See Appendix 1 for more information.

There are some advantages to touring and staying in self-catered lodgings. First, self-catering enables you to spend more time in one area. If you go to Ireland to have a vacation and to relax, this is much easier to do if you sleep in the same bed and stay in the same town for several nights running. Second, by staying in one place for an extended time you are more likely to meet and talk with your Irish neighbors, converse with the local butcher, or pick up travel tips from patrons in the pub.

Self-catering is especially beneficial for large groups and for families. Because most of the homes can accommodate up to eight or ten people, the cost per person goes down considerably. Take, for example, a week's stay in a farmhouse near Doolin with an approximate cost of £300. If six people split the cost, each will pay just over £7 per night. That is considerably cheaper than a night in a B&B, more comfortable than camping, and much more private than a stay in a hostel.

If you take the self-catered option, you can leave all but a daypack at home and travel much lighter than if you had to tour with all your gear. And if you wake up and the weather is especially dreary, you can just turn over and go back to sleep without having to worry about making it to the next destination before the end of the day.

Drawbacks to self-catering include having to take longer rides since you will often end up backtracking. So if the place you want to visit is 35 miles away you'll need to give yourself time to get there and back. For a lot of us, 70 miles of riding eats up most of a day. Second, the sights you came to Ireland to see may not be within a day's cycling distance of your lodging. In this case, you may end up using more trains, buses, or rental cars.

There are some areas of the country where the sights and attractions are clustered closely enough together to make self-catering a viable option. Many of the routes or destinations described in the tour sections of this book lie within reach of self-catered homes.

Campgrounds. The Irish, in general, are fond of camping, and there are a number of caravan parks and campgrounds. (Caravan is the Irish word for camper or trailer.) Be sure the place you plan to stay accepts caravans and tents. Campgrounds are usually located some distance from town and may offer only limited services. Though the rainy days and chilly nights have always deterred me from camping in Ireland, campgrounds are noted in this book whenever they are available.

PUBS. Leprechauns, thatched cottages, shamrocks, St. Patrick, the Church. For better or worse, all of these are seen as part of the soul and character of Ireland. Another institution, one of Ireland's oldest and most revered, is the pub. Public houses are as much a part of Ireland's culture today as they were in the past, and they serve many of the same functions.

Pubs are quite different from most American versions of a bar. There is usually a broader range of people of all ages and fewer people go there just to drink. The Irish, in general, seem to enjoy the pub as the official gathering place for most evenings' conversations.

"Singing pubs" offer nights of traditional ballads and tunes played with such Irish instruments as the fiddle, tin whistle and the bodhran, a type of hand-held drum. In many towns, even those of moderate size, you can probably choose from two or three singing pubs. These lively gathering places provide some of the least expensive nighttime entertainment anywhere, and, though you probably won't be the only tourist, there will likely be a number of local patrons tapping their feet and singing along. And remember: never underestimate the ability of your B&B or hostel hosts to recommend the best place in town.

Though it may seem strange at first, families fit right into many pubs, particularly during the day. In fact, many families go to pubs for lunch, much in the same way Americans would go to the local diner. "Pub grub" is common, and a lot of places specialize in traditional meals. Fare such as fried plaice (a type of fish) and chips, baked chicken with potatoes and cabbage, and other hearty dishes are common in pubs that serve lunch. Note that pubs do not consider sandwiches as lunch. Many pubs do not serve lunch but still serve toasted cheese sandwiches and crisps (potato chips). So even if you miss the lunch serving (usually around 11:30 to 1:30) you can still get sandwiches.

Pubs offer a variety of Irish drinks and brews. Whether by the pint or the half, ales, lager, and stout are generally available on tap. An Irish favorite and an institution in itself is Guinness Stout. This Dublin-brewed dark, syrupy draught forms such a thick head that it takes several minutes for it to settle so your glass can be filled. Its deep, rich flavor inspired a friend to invent the motto, "Never drink a beer you can see through!" If thick and stout isn't your style, try something lighter like a Smithwicks (pronounced *smitticks*), Harp, or any number of locally brewed specialties.

ODDS AND ENDS

If you happen to be toting along anything electrical you'll need to know that electricity in Ireland is 220 volts (50 cycles) which means you'll need a transformer to convert American appliances. The plugs are flat and have three prongs so you'll need the proper adapter to make yours fit.

Here's a list of the official public holidays in Ireland. You'll find that most shops are closed on these days:

> March 17: St. Patrick's Day
> Friday before Easter: Good Friday
> Monday after Easter: Easter Monday
> First Monday in May: May Day Holiday
> First Monday in June: June Holiday
> First Monday in August: August Holiday
> Last Monday in October: October Holiday
> December 25: Christmas Day
> December 26: St. Stephen's Day

Hotels and many restaurants will add a service charge, usually ten to fifteen percent, to the bill. You may tip more if you feel like you got exceptional service. If you're not sure if the tip has already been added, please be sure to ask. Tipping the bartender in a pub is not usually necessary but if you sit at a table, the customary ten to fifteen percent for the waiter/waitress is appreciated.

THOUGHTS ON IRISHNESS. I've never met Darby O'Gill, a leprechaun, or even the typical Irishman—a red-headed, pipe-smoking, superstitious, pub-singing, hard-drinking, Catholic storyteller. No matter what other mental pictures the word Irish brings to mind, you'll likely not find anyone who has all or even very many of those characteristics. Irishness is much too complex to be captured in simple phrases and stereotypes. Qualities and characteristics show up every day and each contributes, in a small way, to describing what I have found the Irish to be like.

To me, Irishness is the shopkeeper who comes out of her store to give directions, starts a conversation about where you're from, and exclaims, "Don't I have an uncle who lives not far from there in Chicago?" It's the gracious, caring attitude of a B&B owner offering a "cuppa" tea and some biscuits (cookies) after your drenching ride to get there. It's the lorry driver who waits, waits, waits patiently instead of passing you on a blind, narrow curve, and then waves as he goes by. It's the voice of the pub entertainer singing a verse of a popular ballad, the noisy bar crowd hushed and attentive. And it's the hostel owner, whose kids end up teaching your kids how to fish for gullies (crabs) out of the local river. And above all, Irishness is not something you buy at a souvenir stand or see on television.

Through the years, the Irish themselves have agonized over their own identity. Beginning with "the troubles" and the six divided counties of the North, the Irish have sometimes struggled to define their place. In the early 1990s Ireland passed the Maastricht Referendum, which placed them more firmly in the camp of European unity. And potential breakthroughs for lasting peace are on the horizon as both Northern Ireland and the Republic of Ireland passed measures in late 1998 supporting cross-border councils to share some of the governance of the North.

Still, it's difficult to see where all of this may lead for Ireland. The mid- and late-1990s have been boom years, as a number of industries, especially those in information technology, have expanded or moved into Ireland. All of this bodes well for employment opportunities and for stemming the tide of emigration from the country. It may also suggest the loss of some of those things that make Ireland a unique place in Europe. Only time will tell if that progress has been worth it.

AN OVERVIEW OF IRISH HISTORY

It's not possible within the confines and context of this book to present a complete account of Ireland's existence. Yet, by knowing at least a little bit of the country's past, you will be more able to understand the importance, significance, and place in history of many of the ruins, castles, and forts you will undoubtedly come across in your travels. With this in mind, this section provides a brief glimpse of Ireland's earliest inhabitants and then digs a little deeper into the Ireland of the past 100 to 150 years. By reading this a couple of times and using it as a reference as you tour, the sites you visit may take on new meaning and, hopefully, you will come away with a more thorough understanding of Ireland's role in history.

WAY, WAY BACK. The last glaciers receded from northern Europe around fifteen thousand years ago. Several thousand years later, around 6000 B.C., humans first crossed over from the European continent into Ireland. These first people belonged to the time archaeologists refer to as the Mesolithic Period, which was part of the Stone Age. Because the island was covered with dense forest, for the next two thousand to three thousand years settlements grew slowly and were confined mostly to open areas around lakes, rivers, and the sea.

By the Neolithic Period (3000–2000 B.C.), agriculture began to take hold as nomads established themselves in one place for longer periods. Besides wild game and forage gathered from the forests, people began to rely more on domesticated animals and, to some extent, grain. A number of the remains of ancient Ireland, such as the great stone burial tombs, date from this time period. Changing climate eventually led to a decrease in forest cover, and around 1000 B.C. civilization began to spread into areas that were at one time too heavily forested.

A Kerryman takes a break with two of his faithful friends.

Around 500 B.C. the Iron Age began and the use of iron in agriculture increased. Farmers became better equipped to break open the rocky ground, and this improved their ability to grow crops. Around this time the early Irish began to build their famous ring forts, which now dot the landscape. In fact, some sources indicate that throughout the country there are over forty thousand of these structures built originally to offer security to large numbers of people. Not only did they keep the inhabitants safe, they also provided protection for livestock that other tribes often tried to steal.

Other groups of this time chose to live in the middle of lakes on floating islands called crannogs. A rebuilt crannog project called Craggaunowen in County Clare is an excellent reconstruction of one of these early sites.

The Celts (pronounced *Kelts*) first began to make their impression on Ireland around 300 B.C. Compared to many European colonizers, little is known about Celtic culture. The Celts developed small settlements, or "kingdoms," and were divided into basically warrior and farmer classes. They added to the country's knowledge and use of iron, and many crafts and stone designs originated with Celtic society. Many of today's Irish trace their heritage back to these ancient people with ruddy complexions and red hair. The Celtic language also came to be used predominantly in Ireland for the next two thousand years.

By the fifth century, Christianity had reached the shores of Ireland and began to make its mark. Monasteries sprang up all over the island, and Christianity spread relatively quickly.

The most successful and certainly the most famous of all Irish priests was St. Patrick. A captive of pagan Irish slave traders, Patrick eventually escaped from Ireland and went to France where he studied to become a priest. He returned to Ireland in A.D. 432. Scholars suggest that he was so successful spreading Christianity because he combined many of the pagan rituals the people were used to with the practices of Christian dogma.

People were drawn to the established monasteries in large numbers because of the monks' leadership in education and in practical matters such as farming. By the seventh century this knowledge helped make cultivation of grains and other plants more common, reducing the population's need for meat and dairy products. With the increase in grains came an increase in the production of spirits, especially ales.

FOREIGN INVADERS. For the next two hundred years or so, all was well in Ireland until the arrival of the Vikings early in the ninth century. These wealth- and plunder-seeking marauders from Scandinavia raided the monasteries, forced many monks to flee, and often destroyed valuable manuscripts. The turbulent seas surrounding the island had lulled many Irish people into believing that their homeland was incapable of being invaded, and they were unprepared for the Norsemen's onslaught. A poem written by an Irish monk demonstrates the prevailing conventional wisdom of the time:

> Fierce and wild is the wind tonight;
> It tosses the tresses of the sea to white;
> On such a night as this I take my ease;
> Fierce Northmen only course the quiet seas.

Unfortunately for him and other monks, this was not to be the case. The Vikings quickly gained access through the rivers that wend their way into the very interior of the country. This let them gain a firm foothold in the country without having to battle their way inland.

As a result of constant invasions, the monks began building tall, round towers to protect themselves and their manuscripts. These towers, some over one hundred feet tall, could only be entered by a door 12 to 15 feet off the ground, accessible by a ladder that could be withdrawn should invaders threaten. A number of these towers still populate the terrain today.

The native Irish did fight back, but their resistance was ineffective until Brian Boru became the High King during the early eleventh century. After winning the famous Battle of Clontarf, the Irish destroyed the Vikings' momentum. Eventually the Norsemen settled in Ireland among their former adversaries. They established villages that soon grew as trade between them, and the Scandinavian countries expanded. Dublin, which was one of the first and largest Norse communities, thrived during this time.

The twelfth century saw the next invasion by a new group of Norsemen, now called Normans, who were ruled by Henry II, King of England. Many areas, such as Dublin and Waterford, were taken over and made to pay tribute to England. However, England did not yet put its full effort into colonizing Ireland and was only able to rule in small areas. Outside of Dublin the Irish were still basically in charge, but were considered a thorn in the sides of subsequent English kings.

As the next two centuries passed, many Irish leaders came to power. In fact, the incomplete domination of Ireland by the Normans led over time to a number of battles and wars over leadership of the island. Many of the great castles that remain today were built by the Normans as defense against the rebellious Irish chieftains.

ENGLISH RULE. In 1366, a series of laws called the Statutes of Kilkenny were passed by the English to subjugate the Irish and to put them in their place. These laws forbade the use of the Irish language, required Irish names to be converted into English, and prohibited intermarriage between Irish and English. Though the decrees were indeed harsh, they actually had little impact. In time the Normans did intermarry and coexist quite well with the native Irish. In fact, over the next two centuries, many of the citizens of Norman descent were on the side of the Irish in the uprisings to come.

"The Rock," seat of Irish power and once home to the famous Brian Boru, High King of Ireland.

In the sixteenth century, King Henry VIII and then Queen Elizabeth ruled Ireland with a firmer hand. Although the Reformation that swept across Europe had begun in earnest by this time in England, the Irish were staunchly Catholic and resisted the imposition of Protestant standards. This initial religious enmity is the real basis for much of the so-called religious warfare that has gone on ever since.

What could have been the ultimate overthrow of the English came in 1602 when the Irish allied with the Spanish. However, because of a number of mistakes and a bit of treachery, the English were able to soundly defeat the Irish in a battle in County Cork. The rout of the Irish led to "The Flight of the Earls," the name history gives to the diaspora of many of Ireland's leaders who left the country and gave up their hopes and claims for an Irish homeland.

Because of the poor economic and social conditions for the Irish who remained, another uprising soon followed. In the mid-seventeenth century Oliver Cromwell arrived from England and with bloodthirsty vengeance put down most of the remaining opposition to the English crown. Defeat became utterly complete for the Irish in the Battle of the Boyne in 1690 when the English, led by William of Orange, defeated James II and his Irish troops. King "Billy" still reigns as a famous hero for a lot of the Protestants of Northern Ireland. This famous victory for their side led to the creation of the Orange Order, to which some of today's Northern Irish belong.

THE STRUGGLE FOR INDEPENDENCE CONTINUES. In the late eighteenth century and during a large part of the nineteenth century, a number of Ireland's most famous and enduring patriots began to exert influence. First came Theobald Wolfe Tone who, in the 1790s, formed an organization called the Society of United Irishmen. His group eventually made two different attempts to rebel against English rule. Both were unsuccessful and after the second, Tone was captured and sentenced to death. Eventually he committed suicide rather than be treated to English justice.

Daniel O'Connell was the next major contributor to the cause of Irish freedom. He was a Catholic lawyer, a position that was indeed unique in a country where most Irishmen were poor tenant farmers. O'Connell, who was to become known as "The Liberator," made self-rule one of his ultimate goals. He was not able to achieve this mark in his lifetime but reforms began to percolate slowly through the system.

Though freedom from English rule was an important part of consistent protests through the years, some of the biggest problems facing the Irish peasants were food production and land ownership. The famine of the 1840s eventually cost the country about two million people, most of whom either emigrated to the United States or starved to death. The failure of the potato crop, the staple food of Ireland's poor, was a primary cause of the mass starvation. Sadly, this tragedy was compounded by the export of available food to increase the profits of English landowners, who controlled most of the arable land.

Most of the Irish farmers leased lands from these often absent landlords who left their estates in the hands of sometimes unscrupulous rent collectors. A number of attempts were made to fix this problem, such as the formation of the Land League and the Land Act of 1870.

Near the end of the nineteenth century Charles Stewart Parnell rose as another champion of Irish Home Rule. He became a member of Parliament in 1875 and worked tirelessly for reform. His many followers called him "The Uncrowned King of Ireland," although he died at the young age of 45 before seeing the fruits of his struggles.

The next several events of Irish rebellion in the face of English oppression unfolded over the early years of the twentieth century. The most acclaimed and probably most important of these was the Easter Rising of 1916. The majority of the fighting that took place over this week occurred in Dublin's streets. A description and summary of the important aspects and the renowned heroes of this uprising follow in Tour 1 under "A Brief History of Dublin."

Though the Easter Rising made champions of a number of the participants, the question of Irish Home Rule was still not settled. For the next five years, through the end of 1920, the quest for independence mounted as guerilla warfare, sometimes open, sometimes discreet, continued in earnest. The dominant political party centered in Dublin, *Sinn Fein* (pronounced *shin fayn* and meaning, "We, Ourselves"), did all it could to see that Ireland became ungovernable for the British.

After countless debates and hours of negotiation, a treaty was signed in December of 1921 to set up the Irish Free State. The agreement gave Ireland the same kind of constitutional status as countries such as Canada, South Africa, and New Zealand. It also included the partition of six counties in the north that opted to remain under full British dominion, a bitter compromise many Irish people found hard to accept.

One other aspect of the treaty was difficult for the Irish to swallow. The oath of allegiance to the King, which members of the Irish Parliament were required to take before being sworn in, caused another schism in an already fractured peace. These two conflicts broke the country into two parts—the pro-treaty forces and the anti-treaty troops, commanded primarily by Eamon de Valera. They soon clashed in a wrenching civil war.

In December of 1922 the last British soldiers left Ireland and the Irish Free State was born. However, it was quite a rocky beginning. The civil war took brutal and often barbarous turns. With the British gone, Irish began battling Irish over the form the new state should take. Finally, by May of 1923, the civil war ended and Ireland began its journey through the constitutional maze that finally produced a home-ruled parliamentary government. The main thorn still left in the side of those opposed to the 1922 treaty is the partition of counties

Home of a former Cromwellian soldier, Parke's Castle now stands as a monument to Ireland's rocky past. Photo by Jeff Kirchhoff

Derry, Tyrone, Fermanagh, Down, Armagh, and Antrim into what is now known as Northern Ireland.

THE CONTESTED NORTH—AN UPDATE. Though the counties of Northern Ireland will, for the foreseeable future, remain as part of Great Britain, some strides have recently been made to quell the violence and to promote cooperation between the peoples of the North and the Republic of Ireland. With assistance from the U.S. government, a plan was brokered which, in mid-1998 was supported and passed by the peoples of both countries. Though the agreement is quite lengthy and involved, some of the key points are:

- The Irish constitution must be amended to remove its claim over Northern Ireland.
- Establishment of a cross-border assembly, with provisions to prevent domination by a likely pro-unionist (pro-union with Britain) majority.
- Establishment of a North-South Ministerial Council to help govern on issues of mutual interest.
- Reaffirmation of participants' commitment to disarming all paramilitary organizations.
- Putting in place measures for speeding up the release of paramilitary political prisoners.

At the time of this writing, a number of the provisions are still being hotly discussed by parties on all sides of the debate. Killings and violence in the name of religion and politics are two things which Ireland would be better off without.

ITINERARIES

If you were to pedal every single mile and see every church, ring fort, dolmen, and ogham stone described in this book you would travel over 1,100 miles and it would take you, if you're an average cyclist, at least a month and a half and possibly two months. Because most of us don't have that much vacation time, the following information suggests what I consider to be the best routes for a two-week, a three-week, and a four-week stay. Though these are broken down into day-by-day schedules, you should definitely feel free to alter, adjust, and otherwise make the tour fit your own plans.

TWO-WEEK ITINERARIES

A TOUR OF THE EAST. One of the two most common arrival points in Ireland is Dublin, and that is where this tour begins. If Irish history is of any interest to you, then the sights of Dublin are a must see. After ample time in the capitol, this itinerary guides you away from the city and into the mountains of Wicklow, where you will find the ancient monastic ruins at Glendalough. Farther south and inland is the wonderfully medieval city of Kilkenny and the imposing Rock of Cashel. This tour culminates in historic Limerick, which is not far from Shannon Airport.

1. Arrive in Dublin
2. Day in Dublin
3. Day in Dublin
4. Dublin to Wicklow (Tour 1)
5. Wicklow to Avoca (Tour 2)
6. Avoca to Kilkenny (Tour 3)
7. Daytrip to Kells
8. Kilkenny to Cashel (Tour 4)
9. Cashel to Tipperary (Tour 5)
10. Tipperary to Limerick (Tour 6)
11. Day in Limerick
12. Day in Limerick
13. Daytrip to Craggaunowen
14. Depart from Shannon

A TOUR OF THE WEST. For those with very limited vacation time, this tour encompasses some of Ireland's best-known and most beautiful sights. After a bus, train, or plane trip from either Shannon or Dublin, this plan begins in the centuries-old city of Cork. Soon, however, you head for the Lakes of

Killarney and the magical Dingle Peninsula. Then you cycle on to Doolin, the Burren, and the city of Galway.

1. Arrive in Cork
2. Day in Cork
3. Cork to Killarney (Tour 7)
4. Daytrip to Lakes
5. Killarney to Dingle (Tour 10)
6. Daytrip to Slea Head
7. Dingle to Tralee (Tour 11)
8. Tralee to Lahinch (Tour 12)
9. Lahinch to Doolin (Tour 13)
10. Doolin to Galway (Tour 14)
11. Day in Galway
12. Train to Limerick
13. Day in Limerick
14. Depart from Shannon

THREE-WEEK ITINERARIES

A BIT OF THE WEST, A BIT OF THE EAST. Day-for-day, this three-week tour of Ireland has more variety than any of the other suggested itineraries. The best of the two-week Tour of the West and the Tour of the East are packed together into this trip. With little or no backtracking, you can go from Cork in the southwest up the western coast to Galway, then by train to Dublin. From here, work to the south along the eastern coast and then progress into the midlands where you can depart from Shannon Airport.

1. Arrive in Cork
2. Day in Cork
3. Cork to Killarney (Tour 7)
4. Daytrip to Lakes
5. Killarney to Dingle (Tour 10)
6. Daytrip to Slea Head
7. Dingle to Tralee (Tour 11)
8. Tralee to Lahinch (Tour 12)
9. Lahinch to Doolin (Tour 13)
10. Doolin to Galway (Tour 14)
11. Day in Galway
12. Train to Dublin
13. Day in Dublin
14. Dublin to Wicklow (Tour 1)
15. Wicklow to Avoca (Tour 2)
16. Avoca to Kilkenny (Tour 3)
17. Daytrip to Kells

18. Kilkenny to Cashel (Tour 4)
19. Cashel to Tipperary (Tour 5)
20. Tipperary to Limerick (Tour 6)
21. Day in Limerick
22. Depart from Shannon

A TOUR OF THE NORTHWEST AND DUBLIN. This proposed itinerary begins in entertaining, lively Galway, and allows enough time to take advantage of its many offerings. The remaining tours traverse rugged, wild scenery such as the Aran Islands, the mountains of Connemara, and the rough, rocky Donegal coast. The latter part of the trip takes you to Dublin, where you can spend several days sightseeing and then depart for home from Dublin Airport.

1. Arrive in Galway
2. Day in Galway
3. Day in Galway
4. Galway to Inishmore (Tour 15)
5. Inishmore to Clifden (Tour 16)
6. Clifden to Westport (Tour 17)
7. Daytrip to Croagh Patrick
8. Westport to Ballina (Tour 18)
9. Ballina to Sligo (Tour 19)
10. Day in Sligo
11. Daytrip to Lough Gill
12. Sligo to Donegal (Tour 20)
13. Donegal to Glencolumbkille (Tour 21)
14. Daytrip to Malin Bay
15. Return to Donegal
16. Donegal to Sligo
17. Train to Dublin
18. Day in Dublin
19. Day in Dublin
20. Depart from Dublin

FOUR-WEEK ITINERARY

MORE OF THE WEST, MORE OF THE EAST. For those fortunate enough to have a full month to tour Ireland, this proposed route has two advantages. First, you can tour Ireland from the south nearly all the way to the north and then take in Dublin. Second, you can do all of this without being rushed or feeling pressured to ride when the weather is bad or when you would enjoy a one- or two-day layover. For stays of longer than a month, be sure to take in Kilkenny and Limerick in the midlands or the Donegal coast in the northwest.

1. Arrive in Cork
2. Day in Cork
3. Daytrip to Cobh and Fota Wildlife Park
4. Cork to Killarney (Tour 7)
5. Daytrip to Lakes
6. Killarney to Waterville (Tour 8)
7. Waterville to Killarney (Tour 9)
8. Killarney to Dingle (Tour 10)
9. Daytrip to Slea Head
10. Dingle to Tralee (Tour 11)
11. Daytrip to Kerry Head
12. Tralee to Lahinch (Tour 12)
13. Lahinch to Doolin (Tour 13)
14. Daytrip to Inisheer
15. Doolin to Galway (Tour 14)
16. Day in Galway
17. Galway to Inishmore (Tour 15)
18. Inishmore to Clifden (Tour 16)
19. Clifden to Westport (Tour 17)
20. Daytrip to Croagh Patrick
21. Westport to Ballina (Tour 18)
22. Ballina to Sligo (Tour 19)
23. Daytrip to Lough Gill
24. Daytrip to Glencar Lake
25. Train to Dublin
26. Day in Dublin
27. Day in Dublin
28. Depart from Dublin

DAYTRIPS FROM SELF-CATERED HOMES

The following list suggests some base locations and some sights you can reach within a day's ride. These combinations work especially well if you stay in self-catered homes.

BASED FROM ARKLOW, COUNTY WICKLOW. These daytrips are dominated by the Wicklow Mountains. Glendalough offers the famous monastic ruins of St. Kevin, while Wicklow Town is known for its beautiful seaside location. The trip to Tullow is on quiet roads and passes through fertile, pastoral countryside.

1. Daytrip to Wicklow (Tour 1)
2. Daytrip to Glendalough (Tour 2)
3. Daytrip to Tullow (Tour 3)

Dramatically and relentlessly, the surf pounds at Ireland's rocky western coastline.

BASED FROM TRALEE, COUNTY KERRY. It would be hard to beat the four daytrips out of Tralee. Despite some difficult, hilly riding, the scenery is unequaled. In addition, Tralee is the home of Ireland's National Folk Theatre.

1. Daytrip to Dingle (Tour 10)
2. Daytrip to Slea Head (Tour 10)
3. Daytrip to Killarney (Tour 8)
4. Daytrip to Kerry Head (Tour 11)

BASED FROM CASHEL, COUNTY GALWAY. Rather than using Galway as a base for touring Connemara, it is possible to use a more central location. By staying in the same place for several nights, you can take in Inishmore (largest of the Aran Islands), Galway City, the picturesque city of Clifden, the astoundingly beautiful Kylemore Abbey, and the town of Cong (where *The Quiet Man* was filmed). *Note:* Be aware that the daytrips in this section are longer than most of those described in this book. Some range from 75 to 100 miles round trip.

1. Daytrip to Inishmore (Tour 15)
2. Daytrip to Galway (Tour 14)
3. Daytrip to Clifden (Tour 16)
4. Daytrip to Kylemore (Tour 17)

BASED FROM DOOLIN, COUNTY CLARE. Whereas the preceding itinerary is for longer-distance riders, this plan should suit low- to middle-distance cyclists. Using Doolin, a hotspot for traditional music, as a base, you can travel by boat to Inisheer (smallest and easternmost of the Aran Islands). Cycling south leads to the Cliffs of Moher and the seaside resort town of Lahinch. To the north is the unique landscape of the Burren.

1. Daytrip to Inisheer (Tour 13)
2. Daytrip to Lahinch (Tour 12)
3. Daytrip to the Burren Display Centre (Tour 14)

BASED FROM WATERVILLE, COUNTY KERRY. The advantage of this itinerary is the range of options it offers. By staying in Waterville on the western tip of the Iveragh Peninsula, you can cycle in several directions, visiting both coastal and inland sites. Many cyclists overlook some of the offerings of the Ring of Kerry because of a lack of time, but a self-catered stay in Waterville gives you the opportunity to see as much as you would like.

1. Daytrip along northern coast of Ring of Kerry (Tour 8)
2. Daytrip along southern coast of Ring of Kerry (Tour 9)
3. Daytrip through center of Iveragh Peninsula (Tour 8)

BASED FROM BUNDORAN, COUNTY DONEGAL. Bundoran is situated roughly halfway between Sligo and Donegal, thus making it a good location from which to explore each town. You can not only wander through Yeats Country near Sligo, but you can travel north to visit the true wilds of Ireland along the Donegal coast. Because of this itinerary's proximity to Northern Island, it is possible to make a detour across the border, although no route for doing so is described in this book.

1. Daytrip to Sligo (Tour 19)
2. Daytrip to Lough Gill (Tour 19)
3. Daytrip to Donegal (Tours 20 & 21)
4. Daytrip to Northern Ireland

A NOTE ABOUT SAFETY

Safety is an important concern in all outdoor activities. No guidebook can alert you to every hazard or anticipate the limitations of every reader. Therefore, the descriptions of roads, trails, routes, and natural features in this book are not representations that a particular place or excursion will be safe for your party. When you follow any of the routes described in this book, you assume responsibility for your own safety. Under normal conditions, such excursions require the usual attention to traffic, road and trail conditions, weather, terrain, the capabilities of your party, and other factors. Keeping informed on current conditions and exercising common sense are the keys to a safe, enjoyable outing.

Political conditions may add to the risks of travel in Ireland in ways that this book cannot predict. When you travel, you assume this risk, and should keep informed of political developments that may make safe travel difficult or impossible.

—The Mountaineers

PART II

21 TOURS GEARED FOR DISCOVERY

Stone ruins are a common roadside sight all over Ireland.

■■

TOUR 1
DUBLIN TO WICKLOW

Distance: 27 miles
Estimated time: 1 day for bike travel, 2–3 days for Dublin
Terrain: Steep hills mixed with flat stretches toward the end

This short tour follows the coast road for much of its length, although for the first several miles there is quite a bit of climbing.

CONNECTIONS. Dublin Airport is reached by air directly from the United States, but planes sometimes stop in Shannon first. To connect from Tour 20 you may fly from Sligo Airport or take a train to Dublin's Connolly Station.

Note: Though Dublin has plenty of accommodations available, I suggest staying outside of Dublin in one of its quieter, less crowded suburbs. One in particular stands out as being a very attractive city close to the bay offering a number of sights of its own to see. *Dun Laoghaire* (pronounced *dun leary*) also has three other features that make it a good candidate for a stay while visiting Dublin: (1) Dublin Area Rapid Transit (DART) commuter trains make frequent runs from there to Dublin and back; (2) accommodations are, in general, less expensive than in Dublin; and (3) since *Dun Laoghaire* is on Dublin's south side, it connects well with the rest of this tour to Wicklow.

Wherever you decide to stay, allow yourself at least three days to see Dublin. You could easily spend an entire vacation here but you can see the best sites in that amount of time. Don't plan on cycling much in the city; though it's not a particularly bad place to ride, it's not particularly good either and the DART and buses make it an unnecessary hassle.

A BRIEF HISTORY OF DUBLIN

Known by its Norse invaders as *Dubh-Linn* (pronounced *duvlin*), meaning "black pool" (because of its position along the dark waters of the River Liffey), Dublin is an almost timeless city with a rich and varied history. Long before the ninth century when the Norsemen crossed the sea to colonize this western outpost, a tribe of people called the Eblani had built a number of settlements along the river. But Dublin's history predates even that, with some of the earliest recorded mention of civilization on Ireland's east coast dating back to the days of the great Alexandrian astronomer Ptolemy during the second century.

Also predating the invasion by the Vikings is the original Irish name of the city, *Baile Atha Cliath* (pronounced *blaa clee*), which literally translated means "town of the hurdle ford." An ancient king, returning from battle, constructed a ford of branches and tree trunks to cross the flooding river, and the name of Dublin has officially been *Baile Atha Cliath* ever since.

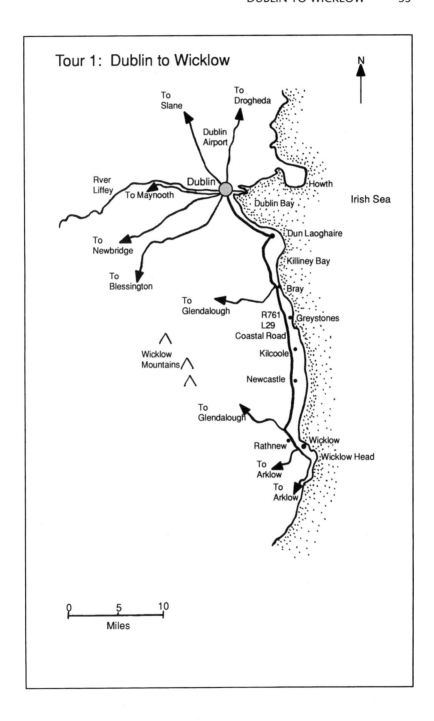

Tour 1: Dublin to Wicklow

N

To
Slane

To
Drogheda

Dublin
Airport

Rver
Liffey

Dublin

To Maynooth

Howth

Irish Sea

Dublin Bay

To
Newbridge

Dun Laoghaire

Killiney Bay

To
Blessington

Bray

To
Glendalough

R761
L29
Coastal Road

Greystones

Wicklow
Mountains

Kilcoole

Newcastle

To
Glendalough

Wicklow

Rathnew

Wicklow Head

To
Arklow

To
Arklow

0   5   10
Miles

The present-day position and design of the city are largely the result of the conquest by the Norsemen. Though a large part of the city has moved to the east, the center is relatively close to where it was originally located. The same thing that has been said about so many of Ireland's many invaders can also be said about the Norse: They eventually became "more Irish than the Irish" as they settled in Ireland, intermarried with the natives, and built homes and villages.

Over the centuries Dublin grew as an established trade connection between Ireland and other parts of Europe. Because of this economic boom, the city grew briskly. Dublin did not fare so well in the next several hundred years. Time after time invaders laid siege to and captured the city. The most lasting and deeply felt occupation was in the latter part of the twelfth century by a new group of Normans led by Strongbow, Earl of Pembroke. Soon after Dublin's defeat, Henry II, a Norman king from England, came to Dublin and awarded the city to the British or "his men of Bristol." Thus "The Pale," the area within the immediate vicinity of Dublin governed by the King's decree, was born. To be "beyond the pale," an expression currently heard in our modern vernacular, was to be outside the confines and protection of the law.

During the seventeenth century, with Ireland firmly under British control, Dublin began a slow, deliberate process of trade and population expansion. However, the quiet times of economic growth were not to last. With Dublin the undisputed capital of the country, it was logical that it became the center of all attempts to establish Irish self-rule. Catholic Emancipation, the Gaelic League, and trade unions all found their roots in the streets and tenements of the struggling city.

A group of cyclists prepares for a ride on a "damp" day.

Then in 1916 came the Easter Rising with nearly a week of heavy street fighting, bombings, and gunboat and artillery fire pouring into the city. Present-day buildings, streets, and monuments bear the names of some of the heroes of the Rising: Pearse, Connolly, Collins, Mallin, MacDermott, and de Valera. Though the rebellion is seen by many as a major turning point in the fight to throw off British rule, all was not yet secure for this city. The Easter Rising eventually led to the treaty with England that many Irish people found unacceptable because it left six northern counties under British rule and forced Irish Parliament members to take an oath of allegiance to the British king. This sparked a bloody civil war between treaty supporters and anti-treaty forces that ended in 1923.

The division between the Republic of Ireland and Northern Ireland continues to be the point on which much of Ireland's politics turns. As mentioned earlier, new progress has been attained in achieving a long-term settlement to the problem. Whether this will result in a permanent cessation of violence and/or the eventual union of the north with the south remains to be seen.

DUBLIN

With a population of nearly a million people, the city of Dublin contains about a third of the country's entire population. Dublin serves as Ireland's political as well as cultural capital, and is truly the only metropolitan area in the country. It is an industrial seaport and an important manufacturer of whiskey, textiles, and beer (particularly Guinness). Encompassing a perimeter of over 50 miles, Dublin is bisected by the waters of the River Liffey and the entire eastern border of the city is formed by the chilly waters of Dublin Bay, which is part of the Irish Sea. The city takes up more than half of the county that shares its name. Ten bridges run from north to south across the Liffey. A number of major roads run into and out of Dublin, including **N11** to the south and **N4** and **N7** to the west. **N1**, **N2**, and **N3** all branch off to the north.

Within the city, most locations are spoken about in terms of where they are in relation to the River Liffey, which runs almost directly east–west for much of its length. So, places are either north of the river or south of the river. The major north–south street is **O'Connell**, which is a multilane boulevard as it runs to the north and much smaller as it heads southward. Actually, after crossing to the south of the river over O'Connell Bridge, the street's name changes to **Westmoreland** and farther on becomes **Grafton Street**, one of Dublin's few pedestrian-only shopping zones.

The **Dublin Tourism Office** is south of the river on Suffolk Street just south of Trinity College. The office is now housed in the restored former church of St. Andrew and is worth a look even if you don't need tourist information. Hours are Monday through Friday 9:15 A.M. to 5:15 P.M. By e-mail they can be reached at information@dublintourism.ie. Their official website is http://www.visit.ie/countries/ie/dublin/index.html (phone 01 850 230330). At the tourist office you can pick up detailed maps of the city and make lodging reservations.

The **General Post Office** is found a bit farther south on O'Connell on the west side of the road. **Connolly Rail Station**, where trains to Sligo and Galway originate, is on **Amiens Street** north of the river on the east side of town. The other station, **Heuston Station**, is on the west end of town on **St. John's Road** near the Guinness Brewery. Trains from Heuston go primarily to the southern destinations of Cork and Kerry. The main **bus terminal** lies just south of Connolly Station on Amiens.

Dublin is home to a number of interesting sights, museums, art galleries, and historic attractions. Fortunately, the city is rather easy to navigate and most of the places described in the following paragraphs are within walking distance of each other. Or Dublin's double-decker buses can take you anywhere in the city you want to go.

For those who have an interest in a particular type of sightseeing, Dublin Tourism has developed three **Heritage Walks** that are walking tours of the city: the **Georgian Trail**, the **Cultural Trail**, and the **Old City Trail**. Each trail uses easily recognizable signage to designate places of importance. Brochures for each of the three tours are available from the Dublin Tourism Office. Taking you through mostly the south part of the city, the Georgian Trail, as the name suggests, pays specific attention to the houses, terraces, and public buildings that are remnants of Dublin's Georgian past. The Cultural Trail includes visits to some of Dublin's grandest architecture and incorporates stops at the **Dublin Writers' Museum** and the **Abbey Theatre**. If the history of Dublin and Ireland is what interests you, then the Old City Trail will be to your liking. Passing through the oldest and most traditional parts of the city, this trail encompasses the **Liberties**, Ireland's oldest section, and two of Dublin's outdoor markets.

For organization and order in seeing Dublin's sights, the city can be artificially divided into four quadrants formed by the intersection of O'Connell Street (running north–south) and the River Liffey (running east–west). Thus, the next sections describe things to see in the northwest, southwest, northeast, and southeast quadrants. All directions within each quadrant are given with the **O'Connell Street Bridge** as a starting point.

The bridge itself is an important attraction. Stationed at the north end, the statue of **Daniel O'Connell** with its four cherubim watches over traffic. The monument also pays homage to several other Irish heroes, including "The Uncrowned King of Ireland," **Charles Stewart Parnell**. Looking west from the bridge you can see the flawless arch of the **Ha' Penny Bridge**, the one pedestrian-only bridge in the city.

NORTHWEST. Two blocks north of the bridge is the **General Post Office** (**GPO**). Most cities don't list their post office as an historic site, but Dublin's definitely qualifies. It was here that the rebels of the Easter Rising made their headquarters. Padraic Pearse, one of the Rising's leaders, announced the creation of the new provisional government from the GPO and posted the famous proclamation of the Irish Republic here. Heavily damaged and nearly burned out during the rebellion, the post office has been largely remodeled and restored. Just past the GPO turn **left** on **Henry Street** and then take the **next right** to the outdoor stalls and carts of the **Moore Street Market**. Looking down the market from the end of the street you will be struck by the melange of bright colors as stand after stand offers bananas, apples, green vegetables, and fresh flowers. Raw pork, fish, and chickens impregnate the air with a potent smell that wafts from the partially enclosed shops lining the

Carved stone crosses tell the story of Ireland's long history.

street. The most peculiar feature of the market is the lines of baby carriages, each displaying a crate of peaches, a box of cassette tapes, bags of apples, or whatever happens to be the bargain of the day.

At the north end of Moore Street **go straight** across Parnell Street into **Parnell Square** to the **Garden of Remembrance**. The centerpiece of the garden is a large cross-shaped fountain surrounded by several varieties of flowers. The sculpture at the west end of the park describes the legend of the children of King Lir. The children's stepmother, Aife, was jealous of the kids so she turned them into white swans. The statue captures the children as they make this transformation. Benches provide a quiet place for thought and reflection away from the bustle of Dublin's busy streets.

North of the garden on the same square is the **Dublin Writers' Museum**. The museum, housed in a restored eighteenth century mansion, displays a history of the literature of Dublin, including original manuscripts, rare editions, and portraits of some of Ireland's greatest authors. Some of the notables honored here are James Joyce, William Butler Yeats, Brendan Behan, and Samuel Beckett. The museum is open from 10:00 A.M. to 7:00 P.M., Monday through Friday in the summer, and Sundays from 11:30 A.M. to 6:00 P.M. There is an admission charge.

Next door to the Writers' Museum is the Hugh Lane Municipal Gallery. This city-owned art gallery houses paintings from a variety of different artists, mostly Irish, and was opened in 1908. There is also an impressive collection of stained glass. Admission to this museum is free. Just around the corner from the Writer's Museum, on Grandby Row is the National Wax Museum. Featuring wax replicas of Irish patriots, entertainers, as well as numerous other celebrities such as Michael Jackson, U2, and Elvis, the museum is a fun way to spend a couple of hours. It is also very kid friendly, so if you've brought children along this really is a must see. The museum is open daily 10:00 A.M. to 5:30 P.M., Sundays from 12:00 A.M. to 5:30 P.M. A reasonably priced admission is charged.

The next stop on this tour of the northwest is St. Michan's Church. Founded in 1095, the church sits on what once was the site of a Danish church associated with an old Danish Saint named Michan. Though there are a number of interesting historical pieces in the church, the main reason it draws such a crowd of visitors each year is because of its burial vaults. Possibly because of dry conditions and constant temperatures the crypts under the church house several mummified remains. The most famous are those of a man said to have been a Crusader, and also those of the Sheares brothers who were executed after the 1798 rebellion. Tours begin at the church office and there is a very modest admission fee. It is also customary to tip the tour guide. To get to the church from the wax museum, travel south down Bolton Street for several blocks as it becomes King Street North. Turn south on Church Street and continue on this nearly back to the river. The church is a block and a half north of the river.

The last part of this tour of the northwest goes to Phoenix Park, one of the largest public parks in Europe. From St. Michan's go south to the river and then travel west along it for several blocks. At the western end of Wolf Tone Quay go north and then follow the signs into the park. Just inside the entrance to the park is the People's Garden, and beyond that are several paths you can take to wander through the beautifully planted and cultivated lawns. Just north of the park is Dublin Zoo (Zoological Gardens), the third oldest public zoo in the world. The grounds of the zoo are as, if not more, beautifully laid out than those of the park. As zoos go, this is a pretty nice one since the majority of the animals are not in cages but exist in more or less a "natural habitat" setting. There's a fairly steep admission charge although families get a pretty good discount. Hours for the zoo are Monday to Saturday 9:30 A.M. to 6:00 P.M., Sundays 10:30 A.M. to 6:00 P.M.

SOUTHWEST. Two blocks south of O'Connell on Westmoreland is the Bank of Ireland, situated on the west corner of the block opposite the facade of Trinity College. Like post offices, bank buildings are not usually registered as historic monuments, but this one has the distinction of having once been the Irish Parliament building. Built in 1729, the chamber inside, which once contained the House of Lords, still boasts its Irish oak woodwork, crystal chandeliers, and antique tapestries. Incidentally, the building fell out of use as a parliament building because the Irish Parliament voted itself out of existence. This is supposedly the only parliament in history to do so.

Go west from the bank on **Dame Street** a block and a half to **Dublin Castle**. The entrance to the castle is behind City Hall. The castle is really a conglomeration of structures. The oldest part is the thirteenth-century **Record Tower** that was part of an early Norman castle. The rest of the building is of nineteenth-century construction. There is an admission charge for tours of the castle. Hours are 10:00 A.M. to 5:00 P.M. on Monday through Friday and 2:00 P.M. to 5:00 P.M. on Saturday and Sunday.

About a block **west** of the castle, on the north side of **Lord Edward Street**, is the recently created **Dublin Viking Adventure**. After a short informative lecture, groups are taken on a series of interactive journeys through the life of **Norse Dublin**. Characters, dressed in period costume, explain the various exhibits and allow you to participate by asking any questions you may have. There is quite a revival in interest in Ireland's Viking heritage and this is just one of several places you can learn more about that history. There is an admission charge and the adventure is open from 9:30 A.M. to 4:00 P.M. daily except for Tuesday and Wednesday.

A bit farther to the **west** at the corner of **High** and **Nicholas Streets** is the exhibit known as **Dublinia**. Upon entering you are given a cassette player and headphones for a self-paced tour of the various reconstructions and artifacts. Dublinia's purpose is to educate about **Dublin's Norse history**, which dates back

Ha' Penny Bridge, a pedestrian-only bridge in Dublin, gives walkers a chance to beat the traffic of the busy streets.

to the late twelfth century. In fact, there are several archaeological digs still continuing in this quarter of Dublin. The Dublinia tour concludes in a walkway over **Wine Tavern Street** but as part of your admission you can continue on into **Christ Church Cathedral**. Christ Church was founded in the eleventh century by a Norse king. Later the church was rebuilt by Strongbow for St. Laurence. Inside is a life-size monument to Strongbow, and in one of the chapels is a container holding the heart of St. Laurence. The crypt underneath the church is also accessible, and a walk through its dank, dusty halls is worth the time.

To lift your spirits after time spent in the cathedral's sepulcher, head west for the **Guinness Brewery Hop Store**. Though separate from the actual brewery, the Hop Store is the part of the establishment that is open to tourists. For a reasonable admission fee you can tour the superb museum, which documents how Guinness stout is made today and how the process has changed through the years. There are several displays of original equipment, a model cooperage (barrel-making operation), and an assortment of other pieces dating back to the brewery's early days in the eighteenth century. The admission price also includes two other worthwhile items: entry into an outstanding audio-visual production that documents the history of Guinness (very entertaining but certainly full of propaganda) and a pint of the dark, rich brew. To get to the Hop Store go west on **Christ Church Road**, which soon becomes **High Street**, and then **Thomas Street**. Stay on this until you reach **Crane Street** where the store is located.

It wouldn't be a visit to Ireland without a stop at **St. Patrick's Cathedral**, located on Patrick Street. The easiest way to get there from the brewery is to hop on a bus, but if you prefer to walk, you can backtrack to Christ Church Cathedral and then turn **south** on **Nicholas Street**. Soon after Nicholas becomes **Patrick Street** you come to the cathedral. Though this particular building has not been here the whole time, one Christian church or another has been on this site since the fifth century. The present structure dates to the twelfth century. Jonathan Swift, author of *Gulliver's Travels*, was dean of St. Patrick's in the early eighteenth century, and he and his wife are both buried here. A publication available inside the cathedral describes some of the various Celtic gravestones and medieval items found inside the church. Besides being open for Sunday services, the cathedral is open to visitors from 9:00 A.M. to 6:00 P.M. Monday through Friday and 9:00 A.M. to 5:00 P.M. on Saturdays. Opening times on Sundays are considerably more restricted. Your best bet is from 1:00 P.M. to 3:00 P.M.

NORTHEAST. In the center of O'Connell a block and a half north of the river, directly across from the McDonald's is a fountain with a sculpture of Anna Livea, who is the goddess of the River Liffey. The statue, a fairly recent addition to Dublin, is jokingly known to the locals as "the floozy in the jacuzzi." The other attraction of note in this quadrant of the city is the **Abbey Theatre**, which is found on the street of the same name. From "the floozy" go **south** on **O'Connell** one block and then **turn left** on Abbey Street. The theater opened in the early twentieth century and soon had its first major performance, *The Playboy of the Western World*, which was written by Irish author J. M. Synge. William Butler Yeats and another Irish playwright, Lady Isabella Augusta Gregory, were the first directors of the theater. Today its mission is primarily to promote and foster new Irish talent and to premier their work.

SOUTHEAST. Follow **Westmoreland** south of O'Connell Bridge three blocks until you come to the unmistakable frontage of **Trinity College**. The brick, colonnaded facade of the austere institution is part of the original college, which dates to 1755. The university was actually founded much earlier and recently celebrated its four hundredth anniversary. Today approximately seven thousand students attend the school, which was first established by the Protestant Church but was opened to students of all religions in the late nineteenth century. Perhaps the most remarkable site on campus is the library with its celebrated **Long Room**. This impressive hall houses some 200,000 ancient books, the most important one being *The Book of Kells*. Made in the eighth century, this is a colorfully and extraordinarily illustrated manuscript of the Gospels of the New Testament. There is an admission charge to the library and lines can sometimes be quite long, but it is definitely worth a stop.

Just a bit south of Trinity is the statue of **Molly Malone**, a fish seller made famous in song.

> *In Dublin's fair city where girls are so pretty*
> *Twas there that I first met sweet Molly Malone*
> *As she wheeled her wheelbarrow*
> *Through street broad and narrow*
> *Crying, 'Cockles and mussels, alive, alive oh'*

Legend has it that she died of a fever and that her ghost now wanders the streets selling her wares.

From the statue turn to the **east** on **Nassau Street** and follow this to **Merrion**. A **right** here takes you the short distance to the **National Gallery of Ireland**. For a tiny country, Ireland has a most impressive collection of fine paintings. Besides a large collection of pictures by several Irish artists, including Walter Osborne, William Orpen, and Jack Yeats, many world-renowned artists are also represented. There are works by Goya, Jan Steen, Pieter Brueghel the Younger, and Rembrandt. Nearly every major school of art is represented in the multifloor building. Admission to the gallery is free.

Right next door is the **Natural History Museum**. If the quality of sightseeing were measured by the quantity of things to see alone, then this museum would win by a long shot. The place is literally crammed with every make and model of critter and beast. While adults may find the place fairly interesting, kids will love it. There's a growling face or furry creature hanging or posed in every nook and cranny.

Sailing has really caught on in the Dublin suburb of Dun Laoghaire.

Down the street a little farther and around the corner to the west on **Kildare Street** is the **National Museum of Ireland**. The museum houses some exceptional pieces of ancient Irish history. Of particular interest are all of the gold brooches, necklaces, and other jewelry that have been recovered from bogs throughout the countryside. The low oxygen content of the soggy ground preserved the pieces, and many of the centuries-old trinkets are in excellent shape. There is a wonderfully informative display describing the events and causes of the Easter Rising and the civil war that followed. You can also sit and watch a movie that details the events of the rising.

Across the street and down a bit from the museum is Dublin's large commons area known as **St. Stephen's Green**. Set aside in the 1600s as a park, the layout of the gardens and lake was completed in the nineteenth century by one of the members of the Guinness family. Hundreds of people, tourists and natives alike, use the park daily for a bit of relaxation from the hectic city pace found just a block or two away.

DUN LAOGHAIRE

The suburb of Dun Laoghaire lies to the southeast of Dublin and sits right on the southernmost point of Dublin Bay. From Dublin city center it is a level 5-mile ride to Dun Laoghaire town center. In Dublin follow the signs that read **Dun Laoghaire/Car Ferry**. This road traces along toward the southeast and passes through **Seapoint** and **Blackrock** before reaching Dun Laoghaire.

In the evening Dun Laoghaire's pier is the busiest place in town. It seems that the residents love to go for their daily constitutional, and the majority of them descend on the long spit of concrete that protects this part of Dublin Bay from the Irish Sea. Besides walkers, there are boys and old men fishing off the walls and street players picking out a tune for 20p here, 50p there. A number of concessionaires with mobile vans sell everything from hot dogs to cotton candy, completing the carnival atmosphere that takes place here nearly every evening. If you visit earlier in the day you may catch a view of children in small boats taking solo sailing lessons. Brightly colored sails skim along as the little sailors tack back and forth behind each other looking like a large snake writhing through the harbor.

To the west of the pier, in a modern chrome and glass building is the Dun Laoghaire branch of **Dublin Tourism** (phone 01 2806984). You can pick up many of the same informational publications here as you can at the office in Dublin. Visible from the pier at the far southeast end of town is the **Joyce Tower**, which James Joyce made famous in his book *Ulysses*. Presently the tower, which was originally built in 1804, houses a James Joyce museum. Inside are many of Joyce's letters, personal possessions, and photographs. The tower is open Monday through Saturday from 10:00 A.M. to 5:00 P.M. and Sunday from 2:00 P.M. to 6:00 P.M. There is an admission charge but it is very reasonable.

DUN LAOGHAIRE TO WICKLOW (27 MILES)

Depending on where you stayed in Dun Laoghaire, or if you did, you need to work your way **south** toward Bray. M11, a motorway (blue sign), is the most direct route, but it is **closed to cyclists.** Instead, take the route marked for **Shankill**, which continues on to Bray. The road is exceptionally hilly, with lots of fast downhill runs and an equally high number of slow uphill charges. At Bray (5 miles from Dun Laoghaire) you enter **County Wicklow**. Bray is a fairly busy resort city and a popular seaside destination. All the normal services and amenities are available. The beach at Bray is over a mile long and there is a 3-mile-long cliffwalk around Bray Head that takes you to the town of Greystones. The **DART** also services Bray, although if you stay here the ride into Dublin is considerably longer.

Through Bray follow the road marked for Greystones, which is **R761 (L29)** but is actually always called **Coastal Road**. The name is rather descriptive since for most of the 5.5 miles (10.5) to Greystones the road does stay within view of the coast.

In 2 miles (12.5) is the small village of Kilcoole. **Continue** on the **Coastal Road** for another 12.5 miles (25) as it passes through the village of Newcastle and goes on to Rathnew. You'll notice that though it is still called the Coastal Road, the route is in fact a considerable distance from the shore. You can see the sea a mile or so in the distance, but the road really goes through farms and pastureland most of the way. This is excellent riding terrain since most of the road is relatively flat. At Rathnew, turn **left** on the road to Wicklow, which is another 2 miles' distance (27).

Thatch and stone are two of Ireland's most traditional building materials.

WICKLOW

The city of Wicklow (*Cill Mhantain*, "Church of St. Manntan") is the primary city in the county of the same name. Wicklow is beautifully situated overlooking the Irish Sea just north of the cliffs of Wicklow Head. There's not a spot in town from which you can't see the ocean, hear its roar, or feel the chilly breeze blowing off it. On the high ridge south of the city are the ruins of **Black Castle**, which are accessible by a path leading along the cliffs. The tourist office is in the center of town on the left side just as the main road forks. Wicklow is large enough to offer services of all types, including a **bike shop**, a number of B&Bs, and an excellent IHH hostel.

Six miles south of Wicklow begins some of the cleanest, most beautiful sandy beaches to be found anywhere in Ireland. Brittas Bay, a popular destination for the locals, gives a good opportunity to soak up the sun and the sand, providing the weather cooperates. Take the main road south out of Wicklow, **R750** (**L29**) to get to the public beach access areas.

■■■■■■■■■■■■■■■■■■■■■■■■■■■■■■■■■■■■

TOUR 2
WICKLOW TO AVOCA

Distance: 30 miles
Estimated time: 1 day
Terrain: Hilly to extremely steep

Though not a long ride, the terrain on this tour is challenging. Most of the ride goes through the Wicklow Mountains, so there are frequent scenic payoffs.

CONNECTIONS. Wicklow is reached after a reasonable 27 miles from the start of Tour 1. There is frequent bus service from Dublin and occasional bus service from Limerick. Trains also run to Wicklow from Dublin's Pearse Station.

WICKLOW TO GLENDALOUGH (14 MILES)

From Wicklow go back **north** the 2 miles to Rathnew on the same road (**R750**) by which you came to Wicklow, but this time continue **straight** to the town of Ashford. Just into Ashford, when you are **4 miles** from Wicklow, take the **left** posted to Glendalough. In another 2 miles (6), turn **right** and climb the **amazingly steep**, nearly 1-mile-long incline through **Devil's Glen**. Once you get to the top and have had a chance to rest, you can look back and see how beautifully forested the road is. However, in all of the times I've climbed it I've found it to be, dare I say, nearly impossible to climb with a loaded touring bike. Three miles per hour is about all I've ever been able to manage before I finally have to give up and walk the last 200 to 300 yards. Congratulations if you're able to complete the climb successfully, still in the saddle and without uttering a torrent of four-letter words. After this, the rest of the trip to Glendalough seems relatively easy and gives you a chance to catch your breath again. At Annamoe, turn left on **R755 (T61)** and continue following the signs to Glendalough. At Laragh, where there is a petrol station/food shop and a couple of pubs, turn right for the last mile (14) to the historic site.

GLENDALOUGH

Glendalough means "Valley of Two Lakes," and in this case they are called **Upper Lake** and **Lower Lake**. Glendalough is set in the heart of what are now the forests and mountains of **Wicklow National Park**. Its fame is due to the well-preserved remains of the monastic site of St. Kevin. Though most of the remains don't date this far back, the monastery was founded in the sixth century. Only a small part of the structures remain, but in the prime years of the settlement the monastery was a center of learning and culture. The majority of the buildings that remain are somewhere between eighth- and twelfth-century construction.

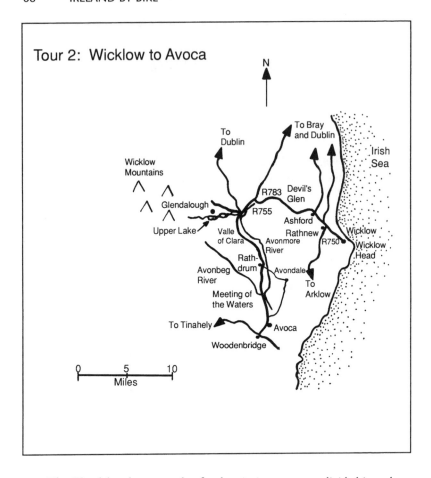

Tour 2: Wicklow to Avoca

The Glendalough area can be, for descriptive purposes, divided into three areas. The first you come to is the **Visitor's Centre**. Inside, there are exhibitions on the history, archaeology, and wildlife of the area. There is also a 20-minute video that shows many of the area's attractions. This is a good introduction to the Glendalough site. There is a small admission fee.

Just down the road a short distance, the two stone arches of **The Gateway** mark what was once the principal entrance to the monastic site. Park your bike here and walk up to the various ruins that are scattered throughout the grounds. In the immediate vicinity you will find the following: (1) **The Cathedral**—the largest building at Glendalough. This structure dates from the twelfth century. (2) **The Round Tower**—nearly 100 feet high. The tower, whose entrance is 12 feet off the ground, was originally divided into six stories. The tower served a dual purpose. It acted as a landmark for visitors coming into the area and became a refuge in times of rather frequent attacks or invasions. (3) **St. Kevin's Kitchen**—one of the few buildings that still has a roof. This building was in reality a church, but because of its chimneylike round tower protruding from the roof, it acquired the kitchen name. A number of ancient headstones and stone crosses are scattered between each of these attractions.

Farther on down the road at **Upper Lake** is **Reefert Church**. The name comes from Righ Fearta, which means "burial place of kings." The church is attractively stationed on a rocky perch in a grove of trees just up from the Poulanass River. The river is fed by the **Poulanass Waterfall**, which is found a short distance up a well-marked trail.

The lake itself is worth the ride. It is snugly surrounded by the Wicklow Mountains and on clear days casts a brilliant reflection. The area is crossed with trails that highlight the natural features of the area along with some more remote remains of St. Kevin's stay here.

GLENDALOUGH TO AVOCA (16 MILES)

To continue on the tour, go **back** the 1 mile to Laragh and turn **right** on R755, which is marked for Arklow/Rathdrum. The 7 miles (22) from this junction to the town of Rathdrum is an incredibly picturesque ride through the **Valle of Clare**. Through breaks in the coniferous forest from time to time you get a glimpse of the **Avonmore River**, which runs peacefully in the valley below. At other times the forest canopy completely closes off the sky and you ride through a literal tunnel of trees. If you're lucky and the rain has turned to a fine mist, the forest takes on a surreal, Tolkien-like quality.

Rathdrum is a town with a number of ordinary services, but its claim to fame is that of being the home of **Charles Stewart Parnell**. Parnell, who was known affectionately by his followers as "The Uncrowned King of Ireland," was an Irish member of the British Parliament. He was an important leader in the Home Rule movement and was also instrumental in bringing land reform to Ireland. A divorce case in which he was personally involved led to his downfall, and he died shortly thereafter in 1891.

If you wish to visit his home at Avondale, **follow the sign** at the far end of Rathdrum and **go straight** across the junction just over a mile to **Avondale**. Cyclists are not charged for admission to the grounds of **Avondale Forest Park**, but there is a charge to tour the house and museum. The grounds are spacious and there are a number of exotic species of trees on the 500-acre estate. The house was recently refurbished, and you can watch an audio-visual presentation on Parnell prior to taking the self-guided tour of the house.

If you make this detour it is possible to work your way back to the Avoca road without backtracking. Simply follow the signs and the road eventually connects back to R752 just south of Rathdrum.

If you don't go to Avondale, turn **right** at the R752 junction just south of Rathdrum and take the road marked for Avoca. In just over a mile you come to a turnoff that connects to Avondale, so you have a second chance to go if you decided not to the first time. On down R752, a wonderful, easy descent of about 6 miles (28) brings you to a **bridge** over the **Avonbeg River**. At the bridge is a stone patio leading down to the river and the **Meeting of the Waters**, the point at which the Avonbeg and Avonmore rivers intersect.

> *There is not in the wide world a valley so sweet*
> *As that vale in whose bosom the bright waters meet*
> *Oh! the last rays of feeling and life must depart*
> *Ere the bloom of that valley shall fade from my heart.*

The poem, by Ireland's National Poet, Thomas Moore, was written under a nearby tree in 1807 to describe this site. The location is not particularly well marked so look for the bridge and a restaurant called The Meetings.

After another 2 miles (30), nestled in the Vale of Avoca, is the scenic village of Avoca. Avoca's renown comes from the presence of **Avoca Handweavers**, Ireland's oldest weaving mill. Turn **left** at the sign for Avoca and cross over the **bridge** into town. In the town center turn left again and follow the road through town and up the steep hill past the church. Avoca Handweavers is about 200 yards past the church. The Handweavers is not a large place, but workers turn out a large quantity of wool sweaters, scarves, hats, mittens, and a number of other handsomely crafted products. The charm of the place is that you can roam about as you like through the buildings and watch as huge skeins of pink, purple, red, and other colors of yarn are masterfully loomed into huge sheets of material. Guided tours are also available at certain times of the day. If you're into wool, it may be hard to leave here without buying. One thought: Many of the products available in the showroom can also be found in the Dublin and Shannon duty-free shops, and you can buy them as you leave the country. That means you won't have to carry them in your panniers for the rest of the trip. Another possibility is to buy them here and have them shipped home.

Abandoned towers and keeps are common fixtures of the Irish countryside. At many you are free to climb and roam around inside.

■ ■

TOUR 3
AVOCA TO KILKENNY

Distance: 59.5 miles
Estimated time: 1–2 days
Terrain: Flat to moderately hilly

The roads for most of this tour can truly be considered backroads. Small villages pop up from time to time, providing timely opportunities to rest or visit a roadside pub. Until you near Kilkenny, the traffic is light and easily managed.

CONNECTIONS. Avoca is reached by bike via Tour 2. You can also get there by train from Dublin or Wicklow.

AVOCA TO TULLOW (30 MILES)

Out of Avoca continue **south** on **R752** just over 2 miles to Woodenbridge where there is another "meeting of the waters." The road from Avoca traces the Avoca River and then at Woodenbridge the river meets the Aughrim River coming in from the west. Turn **right** at the bridge at the signpost for Aughrim. The road is flat and scenic for the next 5 miles (7) as it follows the outline of the Aughrim River for most of the road's length. You don't actually go through the town of Aughrim; a road turns off to the right to go to town if you need to stop for anything. The main road heads on toward Tinahely.

After a bit of average climbing you descend into the town of Tinahely, which is a distance of 15 miles from Avoca. The town resides on the side of a rather steep hill and is resplendently stationed amid the peaks of the Wicklow Mountains. As you climb the hill into town the majority of the shops and services are off to the right. The tour continues on **straight** from here and the road, **R749 (L32)**, is marked for Shillelagh. Fortunately the road seems almost completely downhill most of the next 5 miles (20) to the village of Shillelagh. There are a couple of pubs, a foodstore and restaurant, as well as some lodgings. If you're in Shillelagh in August, you can attend the annual horse fair and farm show. At the crossroad in town turn **right** for Tullow.

There's a bit of moderate climbing from here but it's rather easy terrain through miles of farms and green pastureland. From Shillelagh 5.5 miles (25.5) you climb a short hill and come upon a sign marking a turnoff for **Rathgall Stone Fort**. Rathgall means "hilltop fort," but it's only a short distance up the road and the hill is not very steep.

In 3.5 miles (29), not counting the short jaunt to Rathgall, is a sign indicating your entrance into **County Carlow**. Tullow is only 1 mile (30) from this point. Though not a large town, Tullow has several restaurants, foodstores, and a **bike shop** located just northwest of the town. To get to the shop turn **right** after crossing the bridge over the **River Slaney** and go to the edge of town. The shop is on the right.

If 30 miles is enough riding for you for one day, there are plenty of places to stay in Tullow. And you won't be lacking for things to do. Several pubs in town do a brisk business, and the people in Tullow seem to be exceptionally friendly. Admittedly, not many cyclists find their way through this area, so you're bound to be somewhat of an attraction.

TULLOW TO KILKENNY (29.5 MILES)

The route described in the next several paragraphs is a somewhat round-about course. Rather than intersecting with one of the N or primary roads, the rest of this tour relies mostly on backroads to take you to Kilkenny. *Please read the instructions printed here carefully and check your map often, since there are a couple of confusing crossings to negotiate.*

Just over the bridge at the west end of town, take the **left fork**, which is N81 (T42). This road leads to Wexford, but in 0.5 mile (30.5) go **right** on the road marked for Rathoe. This route winds its way through mostly pastoral farmland and the road is, not surprisingly, narrow. It also sees very little traffic. Stay on this until you come to a small cluster of buildings which is the village of **Fighting Cocks**, 6 miles beyond the turnoff (36.5). There you'll find a junction with a main road. Go **straight** across the main road toward Leighlinbridge (even though you go "straight across" it's actually a slight jog to the **right** for the road going across).

The terrain becomes considerably hillier for the next 4 miles (40.5) until you reach the next junction. Again **go straight through** the junction. In 2 more miles (42.5) you descend a hill and arrive in **Leighlinbridge** town center. The town offers pubs, a post office, and a small foodstore. There is a phone near the stop sign where the road sign arrows point in a number of directions. The road to Kilkenny is **straight** through town. Just over the first bridge (which crosses the **River Barrow**) turn **left** on the lane **marked for Waterford**. This goes for 1 mile (43.5) before another junction with a primary route.

This time turn **left** on N9/N10. At this point the road has two names. For most of the next several miles the road offers an excellent wide shoulder and the terrain is primarily flat with only a few hills of any mention. In 4 miles (47.5) you enter **County Kilkenny** and in another 1 mile (48.5) the road to Waterford forks left. For **N10** to Kilkenny go straight. The wide shoulder extends the rest of the distance through farmland for the next 11 miles (59.5) into Kilkenny town center.

KILKENNY

The **River Nore**, for most of its length, runs north to south through the city. Near the southern extent the river turns east to west, right at the point

Tour 3: Avoca to Kilkenny

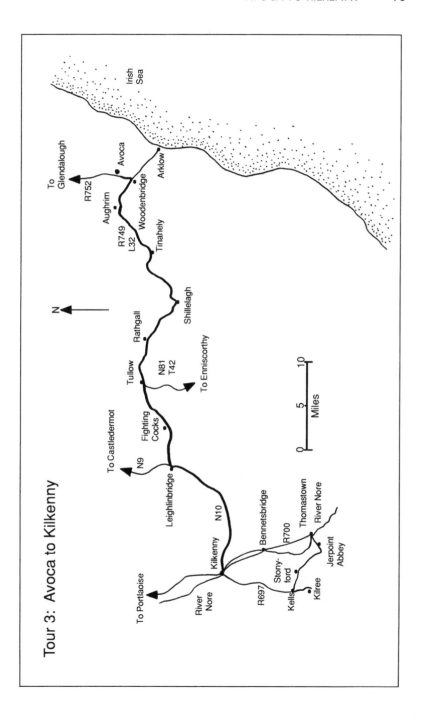

where Kilkenny Castle sits. Two bridges cross the river, one at the north end of town, the other at the south end. At the north, there is **Greens Bridge** and in the south, **John's Bridge**. The main roads going into and through Kilkenny are **John Street**, which runs basically northeast to southwest, and **Parliament Street**, which is on the west side of the river and runs essentially parallel to it. In the middle of town, Parliament divides into **High Street** and **Kiernan Street**.

As you enter town, you soon come to the light at John Street. To the east of this intersection is the **rail and bus station**. If you wish to head to the **tourist office**, turn **left** at the light. Follow this across John's Bridge to the *"i"* (phone 056 51500) on the right side of the road. Just down the road and to the **left** are **public toilets**. The **post office** is around the corner from the *"i"* to the right, up High Street. The majority of the shops and businesses are on the west side of the river along Parliament, High, and Kiernan streets.

Kilkenny has a fine aristocratic heritage that tended to revolve around two Norman families, namely the Earls of Desmond and the Butler Earls of Ormond. It was here that the infamous **Statutes of Kilkenny** were passed in 1366. These ordinances outlawed the intermarriage or assimilation of those of Norman descent with the Irish. Though the law was rigid it became very difficult to enforce; so many of the inhabitants were already of mixed blood. (Once again the Normans had become "more Irish than the Irish.") Kilkenny is truly a medieval city that has retained much of its ancient character and original layout. The streets are narrow and the storefronts are packed tightly together. Numerous arched lanes branch off the main streets, and here and there ancient stones serve as reminders of the original town plan.

If the Middle Ages laid the foundation of Kilkenny's past, then without a doubt the game of hurling is the spirit of the present. It is unequivocally the game of choice for the residents of this city. Not only are the citizens devout followers of the County Kilkenny hurlers, but they play the game constantly. They play it in school, in sandlots, and in hurling "Little Leagues." A sure way to start a conversation in a Kilkenny pub is to ask something about hurling. Maybe you could inquire about an upcoming match. Or, if you're like me, you'd like to have the scoring explained to you. Whatever the case may be, a good question about hurling will start the conversation flowing for sure. As you will likely be told, the finer points of hurling require power, skill, and finesse. The saying goes like this: "Hurling is a game for piano tuners. Football (Gaelic) is a game for piano movers."

If you are lucky enough to be in town for a hurling match at the stadium, see what you can do about getting tickets. For raw enthusiasm and spirit, there's nothing quite like the excitement of a Kilkenny hurling crowd. Matches are held at **Nowlan Park**, which is to the northeast of the city past the rail and bus station.

Kilkenny's medieval past offers a number of attractions for visitors. The

Kilkenny Castle, a thirteenth-century landmark, has been restored to much of its former glory. Photo by Jeff Kirchhoff

former home of the Butler family, imposing **Kilkenny Castle** sits majestically above the city on the banks of the River Nore. The castle was built in the thirteenth century and was added to and remodeled over the centuries. Actually, the site on which the castle sits was prominent in Irish history before this. It was one of many places conquered and settled by the followers of Strongbow, Earl of Pembroke in the 12th century, during the Norman conquests of Ireland. At different times both William of Orange and James II (whom William defeated at the Battle of the Boyne) were guests here. The castle has been well restored and the work continues. Many of the rooms have been refurnished with the original pieces that were sold off at auction during the late 1930s. About the same time the castle was sold to the city for 50 pounds. You must go with a tour group through the castle; individual browsing and photographs are not allowed. Tours, which begin with a short video about the castle, leave frequently from the main entrance. There is an art gallery and a tea room in the basement. The castle is open daily from 10:00 A.M. to 7:00 P.M. The castle is closed on Mondays, except during the summer. The admission charge is reasonable. The grounds surrounding the castle are quite expansive, especially in back of the castle. On the north side, stairs lead down to a marked path that takes you along the shady banks of the river. Admission to the grounds is free, and they are open until dark.

Kilkenny Design Centre is located directly opposite the main entrance of the castle. Its several buildings occupy the old stables and coach houses of the castle that were built in 1760. The rooms have been nicely refurbished, and they house several Irish craftsmen. You can buy a variety of crafts here such as pottery, sweaters, and crystal. You can also have purchases shipped directly home if you like.

Dominating the center of the business district is the **Tholsel**, Kilkenny's City Hall. The structure dates back to 1761 but was destroyed by a fire in 1987 and has since been completely redone.

Rothe House, located north of the Tholsel on Parliament Street, was built in 1594 and was the home of a Tudor merchant. Currently it is the headquarters of the Kilkenny Archaeological Society and houses a museum and period costume collection. The house is open Monday to Saturday from 10:30 A.M. to 5:00 P.M. and on Sundays from 3:00 P.M. to 5:00 P.M.

The Smithwick's Brewery (pronounced *smitticks*) is located next door to the **Irish Budget Hostel** on north Parliament Street. Smithwick's is a Kilkenny-brewed beer but the company is actually owned by Guinness. Technically, the brewery is also called **St. Francis Abbey Brewery** after the monks who began brewing ale during the fifteenth to seventeenth centuries. You can take the so-called tour of the brewery, which is actually just a fifteen-minute video with free samples afterward. The video and sampling are free but you must get a ticket beforehand at the *"i."* There is only one tour per day and it is limited to 50 people. Children under 14 are not admitted, even with parents.

The name Kilkenny in Irish is *Cill Chainnigh*, which means "Church of Canice," and the town and county's namesake is located here. **St. Canice's Cathedral** and **Round Tower** are found at the far north end of town where Parliament meets **St. Canice's Place**. The round tower is one of the most outstanding attractions in the city and is a must if you visit Kilkenny.

The cathedral was built in the thirteenth century and sits atop a hill overlooking the city. The current structure is the product of a number of renovations; services have been held at this site since about the sixth century. Inside are numerous monuments, plaques, and chapels which commemorate the dead of seemingly countless Kilkenny families. On the same grounds stands the 100-foot-tall round tower, which is one of the few in Ireland you can enter. For a very small fee you can ascend the ladderlike stairs as they wind their way to a number of wooden platforms. If you're acro- or claustrophobic you may be uncomfortable making this trek. You will be completely enclosed in the stone tower until you reach the top, where there is a fabulous view over the entire city. It looks out over the gray, peaked roofs that line the curvy streets. You can also see Kilkenny Castle in the distance.

DAYTRIP TO KELLS (31.5 MILES ROUND TRIP)

Head south out of Kilkenny on **Patrick Street** toward Waterford. In 0.5 mile turn **right** on **R697** for Kells. In a short distance, follow the signs to Kells **straight** through the roundabout. A nice level ride through gentle farmland leads for 9 miles (9.5) to the village of Kells. At the junction in town turn **left** at the sign to Thomastown. A little farther up the road on the left you will see the expansive remains of **Kells Priory**, which dates to approximately the thirteenth century.

The best view of the overall arrangement of the priory is from this side as you ride up toward the carpark. There's no admission charge to the grounds. In fact, you'll likely be one of the few people visiting the site. Only a local herd of sheep patrol the area, which covers most of five acres. The whole enclosure is walled and stone turrets guard the corners. In the northern part of the complex you will find the remains of the church and the monastery. You can wander around, climb on the exposed inner walls, and generally make yourself at home. This is one of the most impressive sets of ruins described in this book and if you are anywhere near Kilkenny, it is definitely worth the effort to see it. The County Kilkenny guide (see Appendix 1) sums it up best when it says, "If County Kilkenny were not packed with riches, Kells ... would form a showpiece around which a tourist industry would develop by compulsion of impact."

From the carpark at Kells follow the sign to **Kilree Church** and **Round Tower**, which is 1.5 miles (11.5) down the road and worth a look. The tower no longer has a top but the entrance is low enough to the ground that you can climb up and have a look inside. The inside of the church has two very nice stone arches and probably dates from around the 10th to 11th centuries. The best thing about this site is its seclusion in a dense clump of trees in the middle of a pastured field. There's also an inscribed stone cross in the field about 30 paces from the round tower. You can't miss the round tower as you approach from Kells, but there's no sign at the entrance, just a gate and a stile.

Backtrack from here to Kells and turn **right** toward Thomastown. In 1 mile (14) turn **right** at the crossroad in the village of Stonyford. Through town go **left** on the road to Thomastown. The road is a bit hillier until the next junction, which is 4 miles away (18). Turn **left** here toward Thomastown. This road is **N9** and will likely be considerably busier. Another mile (19) brings you to **Jerpoint Abbey**, founded in 1158 by the King of Ossory, Donal MacGillapatrick, for the Benedictine monks. Since then it has been carefully restored. There are a number of intricately carved stone arches surrounding the abbey as well as a variety of sculptures of saints and knights on the walls and tombs. For most of the summer the hours are 9:30 A.M. to 6:30 P.M. daily. The exception is from May to mid-June when the abbey is closed Mondays and has slightly reduced hours the rest of the days of the week. There is an admission charge.

Continue north on **N9** for another 1.5 miles (20.5) to the town of Thomastown. This is one of the two places on the return leg of this daytrip that has a scenic crossing of the River Nore. In Thomastown follow the signs to Kilkenny as the road winds a path through town. The road is **R700**, and in 5 miles (25.5) you enter Bennetsbridge, where there is another crossing of the Nore. After another 6 miles (31.5) of fairly level riding you enter Kilkenny. From this entrance into town you can see what is left of the medieval walls of the city. The road comes back into town on **The Parade**, the road that takes you in front of the castle's main entrance.

■ ■

TOUR 4
KILKENNY TO CASHEL

Distance: 35 miles
Estimated time: 1 day
Terrain: Flat in the beginning, becomes hilly during latter half

Another relatively short tour, this route takes you from the busy Kilkenny area through the quiet villages of the Slieveardagh Hills. The final miles of the tour bring into view the Rock of Cashel, one of Ireland's most celebrated fortresses.

CONNECTIONS. By bike, Kilkenny connects directly from Tour 3. Kilkenny is reached by train from Dublin and from Limerick, though the route is somewhat roundabout. Plane connections are possible from both Shannon and Dublin airports.

KILKENNY TO CASHEL

Leave Kilkenny toward the southwest on **N76**, following signs for Clonmel/ Callan. The next stretch is an easy ride but the road is rather busy with only an intermittent shoulder. In 6.5 miles, turn **right** on **R691 (T37)**, which is marked to Ballingarry. The road is level and a very simple ride all the way to the **County Tipperary** border, which is 6 miles (12.5) beyond the turn. Continue following the signs to Ballingarry and Cashel. In 2 miles (14.5) the road begins a slow, but steady climb along the **Slieveardagh Hills**, and after 2 miles (16.5) of climbing, you reach the hillside hamlet of Ballingarry, which is perched at the top of the ascent. There is a foodstore, public phone, and little else.

After passing through town the road makes a steep, fast descent and you lose all the altitude you gained by climbing up to Ballingarry. The way from here becomes very rolling and has several challenging hills for the next 7 miles (23.5) to the village of Killenaule. There are only a few more services here than in Ballingarry. One site worth stopping at is the Catholic church, which is built in a classic Gothic style. From here the road climbs several scenic, pastoral hills to the town of Laffansbridge (26). In 9 miles (35), you come to Cashel. As you enter town, look to your right to get a good view of the **Rock of Cashel**, the city's most famous landmark.

CASHEL

At the first stop sign turn **right** toward the town center and the majority of businesses. At the next turn, go **left** about a block to the *"i."* You can pick up information about the Rock and a County Tipperary guide if you don't already have one. There is camping not far from the Rock, and all other services, including **bike repair**, and an IHH hostel are available.

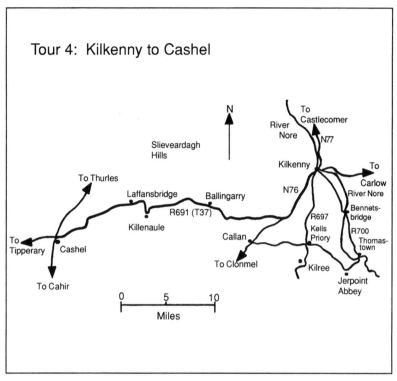

Tour 4: Kilkenny to Cashel

Though a fairly small town, Cashel (the name means "stone fort") offers a variety of things to see and do. The most obvious and most popular attraction is the Rock of Cashel, which is perched royally on the knob above town. It is also called St. Patrick's Rock because the famous saint spent several years preaching and baptizing here. The complex is actually a collection of several buildings that date from the twelfth to the fifteenth centuries. The whole compound was walled in during the nineteenth century. Though the remaining buildings are up to eight hundred years old, the site has been a place of power since the fourth century, and possibly earlier.

No description can adequately convey the awe inspired by this massive rock that looms 300 feet above the Tipperary plains. Go off a distance on the road to the north for a full view. (Incidentally, this is the same view that many travel publications and tourist bureaus use in their informational brochures.) From the summit around the castle you also get a good look at how the town of Cashel is laid out, and you can see a couple of other attractions as well. Hours of operation are daily from 9:30 A.M. to 5:30 P.M. from March to mid-June and 9:30 A.M. to 7:30 P.M. from June to September. There is an admission charge.

Ireland's famous High King, Brian Boru, was crowned here in the latter part of the tenth century. Later he became High King or Imperator Scotorum

(Emperor of the Gaels). Cormac McCarthy, King of Munster, ordered much of the early construction and is especially known for the tiny Romanesque chapel that is now named for him. Fairly recently, ancient frescoes were uncovered by archaeologists. The frescoes were covered in plaster to protect them from being destroyed by Oliver Cromwell and his invading armies. At the time of this writing they were still being uncovered by archaeologists using needles, brushes and scalpels. The rest of the structures, the cathedral, the round tower, and the living facilities were added through the years. The museum inside one of the restored buildings contains a number of ancient relics, including Bronze Age tools and a fourth-century stone used for the coronation of kings.

A short distance to the west of the rock is **Hore Abbey**, a Benedictine and later Cistercian monastery with a cathedral nearly as grand as the one on top of the hill. The grand arches and intact stone roof are prime pieces of architecture. From inside the abbey you also get a well-framed view of another aspect of the rock's grandeur.

In town, not far from the *"i"* is another well-preserved artifact, the **Abbey of the Dominican Order**. It dates to the thirteenth century. If you want to wander through it you must get the key from a nearby resident. The address is on the gate.

For an evening of excellent entertainment there is the **Bru Boru Theatre,** which features traditional Irish music, songs, and dance. This folk theater offers performances nightly at 9:00 from Tuesday through Saturday. After the show the audience is invited to a less formal setting and can participate in the singing and even learn how to do some of the amazing Irish "step dancing" (you know, the "Riverdance" stuff). If you feel like splurging, try the pre-show banquet that is often available. The theater is located near the entrance to the Rock of Cashel. Although generally not necessary, except during late July or August, the number for reservations is 062 61122.

The Rock of Cashel would have been an awesome sight for the monks looking out a window of their eleventh-century abbey.

■■

TOUR 5
CASHEL TO TIPPERARY

Distance: 32.5 miles
Estimated time: 1 day
Terrain: Flat at the start, becoming very hilly near the end

This tour takes full advantage of Ireland's varied scenery and sights. Near the beginning you can take in a thirteenth-century castle; toward the end you encounter challenging climbing through the Galty Mountains. For much of the trip, the route follows uncrowded roads through the lovely Glen of Aherlow.

Looking at any map of Ireland you will quickly notice that the distance between Cashel and Tipperary is not 32.5 miles. This tour takes advantage of additional scenery and less crowded roads instead of opting for an "as the crow flies" approach. However, you could easily cut the distance between Cashel and Tipperary by taking **N74 (T36)** directly from Cashel to Tipperary, which is a trip of only 11 miles. Toward the west end of Cashel take a right turn and then an immediate left and follow that road the entire distance to the town of Tipperary. The main disadvantage of following that route is that you will miss the excellent castle in Cahir. But if time restraints dictate it is certainly an option.

ALTERNATE ROUTE FROM CASHEL TO LIMERICK (35 miles). If your trip is nearly over at this point, and you are getting short of time, there is a much more direct route from Cashel to Limerick, near Shannon Airport, than by following Tours 5 and 6. These tours take you to a few more ruins and through some fine scenery, but if time is of the essence you can follow the much shorter route described in the next couple of paragraphs. Even still, this route stays on true backroads for most of its length, only getting onto a primary road within a few miles of Limerick. While this makes for great, traffic-free cycling there are also very few services available along the way.

To take this **alternate route**, head **north** out of Cashel on **R505 (L111)** toward Dundrum which is a distance of about 9 miles and has a nice crossing of the **River Suir**. The road a few miles on either side of Dundrum has some of the hilliest parts of the ride. Through Dundrum **follow the signs** for Cappagh White, which is still on the same road and 4 miles (13) distant. In 5 more miles (18), still on **R505 (L111)**, you cross the border into **County Limerick**. In another mile (19) you pass through the tiny crossroads of Doon.

From here it is another 4 miles (23) to the small cluster of houses called Cappamore. An additional 5 miles (28) take you to the primary road leading from the **south** into Limerick, N24. Turn **right** onto N24. For the next couple of miles (30) the road has a decent shoulder, something you will appreciate because there is steady traffic. However, after that, the next 5 or so miles (35) to

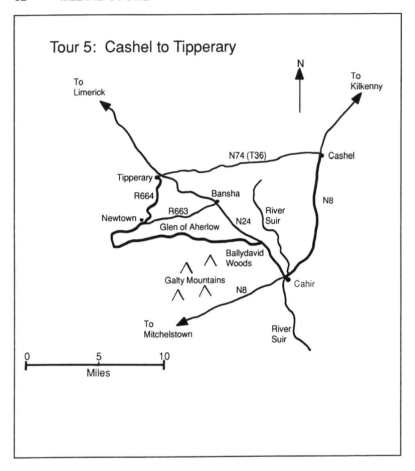

the outskirts of Limerick the shoulder disappears and, because of the traffic, riding can be rather tense.

For more information on Limerick, please skip to near the end of Tour 6.

CONNECTIONS. By bike, Cashel is reached by following Tour 4. Because there is no train service into town, the second-best method to get there is by bus from Limerick. Cashel is a common stop for the Irish bus lines.

CASHEL TO CAHIR (11 MILES)

At the west end of Cashel turn **left** on N8 to Cahir. This is a very nice route and the road is fairly level. The shoulder is also reasonably wide and smooth. In 8.5 miles turn left for Cahir on **R670.** The town center is 2.5 miles (11) farther up this road. In town you will find B&Bs, a hostel, and camping.

At the **first junction,** turn **right** to **Cahir Castle.** There is a parking area on the left across the river from the castle. Much of the castle dates from the thirteenth century, and an extensive amount of restoration has been done. The castle sits on an island of rock right in the middle of the River Suir. At one time this would have been a strategically important setting, but today the river is not deep enough to prevent an onslaught. Tourists arrive daily to storm the castle and stroll inside its keep.

Because of the refurbishment, much of the castle is made to look as it would have several centuries ago. The cobbled courtyard adds an extra dimension of authenticity, and the heavy oak doors must have provided secure entry at one time. Perhaps the most interesting feature is the large number of circular stairways you can climb to take you into turrets, antechambers, and larger halls. In many of the larger rooms, exhibits demonstrate some aspects of life in the

An intricately carved arch is nearly all that remains of this once elaborate church.

castle. A sobering climb down a set of stairs takes you to the dank remains of a dungeon, complete with water dripping from the dark walls.

Included in the small admission charge is a 20-minute audio-visual show that gives some of the background about the castle. The castle is open during the summer from 9:00 A.M. to 7:30 P.M. daily.

CAHIR TO TIPPERARY (21.5 MILES)

Beyond the castle, on the right is N24 to Tipperary/Limerick. As you pedal out of town on this road, you can see ahead to the **Galty Mountains** along whose base this road skirts. In 4.5 miles (15.5) turn left on the small road to **Glen of Aherlow**. Once again the tour leaves the busier primary route in favor of a less crowded, more scenic way.

In just under 2 miles (17.5) you see a sign to the left for an IYH hostel near the **Ballydavid Woods** by which this road passes. The glen, or valley, travels along the base of the mountains, and you can see the verdant slopes of several peaks with enchanting Irish names. As you go along there are **Slieveanard, Sturrakeen, Knockastakeen, Slievecoshabinnia**, and, the highest of all at just over 3,000 feet, **Galteemore**. To the north of the road for some of the distance is the **River Aherlow**, which is partially fed from the runoff of mountain tributaries. In 7.5 miles (25) from the turnoff, turn right on the road to the north following "The Glen" signs. In just less than 1 mile (26) at the next crossroads, take the **right** to Bansha. You stay on this for only 1 mile (27) and then, not long after you pass "The Glen" Hotel, you turn **left** on **R664** to Tipperary.

The first indication that a climb lies ahead is the sign warning that the road is not safe for horse caravans. For about 1 mile (28) the road climbs **very, very steeply**, to a hairpin turn where the **Statue of Christ** is located. This is an excellent spot to take in the green, rustic beauty of the glen below. It's also a good place to catch your breath since the road continues its abrupt ascent for another 1 mile (29) from here. This 2-mile climb goes up **Slievenamuck Ridge**, which borders the north side of the glen. At the top of the hill you begin a lightning-fast, mile-long descent (30) that finally levels off for the last 2.5 miles (32.5) into Tipperary.

TIPPERARY

At the first stoplight upon entering town turn **left** on **Main Street** and then take a **right** at the next turn on **James Street** to get to the *"i."* The **post office** is up a little farther on James Street on the right.

The town gets its name from the river that flows just south of here, the **River Ara**. The Irish name is *Tiobraid Arann*, which is translated as "Well of Ara." Though Tipperary is the namesake of the entire county there is not an overwhelming number of attractions in Tipperary and its well no longer exists. As an overnight stay it has plenty of services, including B&Bs, restaurants, pubs, and a **bike shop.** And as the locals like to say, "Take a trip to Tipp, it's not a long way." Of course this disagrees with what Englishman Harry Williams said in verse in the early part of this century:

> *"It's a long way to Tipperary*
> *It's a long way to go*
> *It's a long way to Tipperary*
> *To the sweetest girl I know."*

Since it's only 32.5 miles from the last tour, you decide.

■ ■

TOUR 6
TIPPERARY TO LIMERICK

Distance: 32.5 miles
Estimated time: 1 day
Terrain: Rolling ground interspersed with occasional steep hills

Enjoy the quiet country surroundings at the outset of this tour. The miles take you to a fine collection of prehistoric ruins. Soon after departing the archaeological site, you begin to enter the brisker flow of traffic heading to the bustling city of Limerick.

CONNECTIONS. By bike Tipperary is best reached by following the route of Tour 5. It can also be reached easily by bus from Limerick.

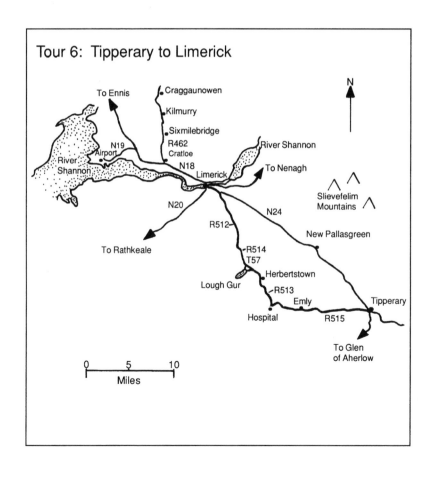

The sprawling, restored ramparts of King John's Castle in Limerick command a view of the River Shannon.

TIPPERARY TO LOUGH GUR (20.5 MILES)

Head **west** out of Tipperary following the signs for Cork that are just past the **Maid of Erin** monument. In a short distance **veer right** at the next road marked for Killarney. This road is also known as the **Emly Road**, and you reach Emly in 8.5 miles after a gently rolling ride. Through Emly turn **right** on R516 (T57) to Hospital. The route is now a bit more challenging but not difficult.

In 3.5 miles (12) you arrive in the town of Hospital. The town's odd name comes from the **Knights Hospitallers of St. John of Jerusalem**, which was founded in 1215. Turn **right** in the town center and head toward Limerick on R513 (T50), which takes you 4.5 miles (16.5) to the crossroad in Herbertstown. Actually you don't go into the town itself; instead you continue **straight** and in just another mile (17.5) turn **left** on the road to **Lough Gur**.

In 1.5 miles (19) the road turns to the **right** and goes another 1.5 miles (20.5) to Lough Gur. The entrance road veers to the **left**.

Lough Gur is the site of prehistoric megalithic remains that date as far back as 3000 B.C. At the entrance to the lake and visitors center there is a map that shows where the artifacts are located and explains the significance of each of the sites. The visitors center itself is done in a style similar to the type of construction that may have been there at one time. The buildings, complete with cone-shaped, thatched roofs, house a museum, an audio-visual presentation, and an information office.

Not all of the archaeological sites are found on the route described in this tour, although **Bouchier's Castle**, which dates from the fifteenth century, and some early circular forts can be seen near the entrance to the lake. For more information about additional spots around the lake, inquire at the visitors center.

LOUGH GUR TO LIMERICK (12 MILES)

To continue to Limerick go back out the entrance and take an **immediate left**. The road is narrow, unsigned, and a **tough climb** for a short distance. The road widens in just over a mile (21.5), and this takes you to the junction with **R512** (24.5). Take the **right** turn to Limerick, which is an easy 7 miles (31.5) away. The road widens here, but it also gets considerably busier. When you near Limerick you will encounter **two roundabouts**. Go **left at the first roundabout**, which is marked for Cork/Tralee. After another mile (32.5), at the **next roundabout**, take a **right** to the city center.

LIMERICK

Because of its size and proximity to Shannon Airport, Limerick is a hub of activity from all parts of Ireland. From here **N18** goes out northwest to the airport and to Ennis and to Galway, **N69** goes to Tralee, **N7** goes to Dublin, and **N24** goes to Waterford.

Though only about half the size of Cork, Limerick has a lot to offer and is spending a good deal of money and effort to upgrade its riverfront appearance. Most of the businesses, sights, and services the tourist needs are located south and east of the River Shannon. The major thoroughfare that runs nearly due north–south is O'Connell Street, one way for most of its length. At the northern end **O'Connell** is called **Patrick Street**. Two bridges cross the river near the city center. The one farthest east is the **Sarsfield Bridge**, the older of the two bridges. The other, **Shannon Bridge**, is wider and carries more of the airport/Galway traffic. A third, **Nicholas Street Bridge**, crosses the river to the northeast of the city near King John's Castle.

The *"i"* is in a bright, modern building very near the River Shannon. Since many of the streets downtown are one way, you have to take a somewhat oblique route to get there. As you near the center, turn **right** on **Wickham Street** or **High Street**. Follow this **three blocks** and turn left just after the **Milk Market**. Stay on this street until it intersects with **Patrick Street**. Turn **left** here and then make an **immediate right** and you'll see the glass and canopy of the *"i"* (phone 061 317522).

The **Rail and Bus Station** is at the opposite end of town on **Parnell Street** near where you came in from Lough Gur. For the **General Post Office** follow **Patrick Street** south until you turn **right** on **Lower Glenworth Street**. Turn **right** again on **Henry Street**. The GPO is on the corner to the right.

If you'd like to stay out of the city center but within walking distance of it, a number of B&Bs are located just across the Sarsfield Bridge on what is called the **Ennis Road**. Right across from the *"i"* is a new indoor shopping center called **Arthur's Quay**, and a variety of shops of every kind are located within a three or four block radius.

Close to 80,000 people live in this town, which has its origins as a tenth-century Viking settlement. Because of its position on the shores of the River Shannon, Limerick soon attracted a considerable amount of commerce and its population burgeoned. In the twelfth century the Normans took over Limerick and established themselves, as they did in many other locales, as essentially Irish rulers. By the sixteenth century the British decided to take firmer control of their lands in Ireland. This set off the first of several major wars in which Limerick played a part. The ruling Norman families, especially the Fitzgeralds, resisted English domination in what came to be known as the **Geraldine War**.

Oliver Cromwell was finally successful in subjugating Limerick after a long and intense siege during 1651. The **Treaty of Limerick** was signed after the **Jacobite-Williamite War** of 1689, but its terms were never fully honored by the British. Even today, the city of Limerick is known as the City of the Violated Treaty.

Through the succeeding centuries, Limerick gradually grew as first its agricultural base and then, more recently, its industrial base began to grow. Perhaps the biggest boost to the local economy was the construction of Shannon Airport, which is only about 15 miles from downtown Limerick.

Though one guidebook has called Limerick a "large, but dull city," there are a number of both historic and contemporary attractions to see. And because of its closeness to Shannon Airport this is a great place to recover from jet lag or to make your preparations for a trip home. If you have time you can easily spend a couple of days here walking the city and taking advantage of its many offerings.

King John's Castle is upriver from the *"i"* just around the bend of the river on **Nicholas Street**. The thirteenth-century castle, built around the time of the Norman invasion, has undergone extensive renovation and has an outstanding exhibition and audio-visual presentation. The exhibition area is decorated with the banners and tapestries of medieval times and explains chronologically the history of both Limerick and the castle itself. The displays are so informative and so complete that if you read every word your head will probably ache from all the detail.

You can also wander about the heavily fortified stronghold, antechambers, and towers as well as the courtyard. Excavations underneath the main buildings reveal evidence of a settlement built prior to the castle's construction. The castle was in nearly constant use for almost five hundred years, practically a record for oft-besieged Irish castles. The admission charge is rather steep but well worth it. There are family and group rates available.

The **Treaty Stone**, the place where the treaty ending the 1691 siege was signed, is found across the river from the castle. Go west across the nearby bridge and take a **left** on the first street after it.

St. Mary's Cathedral is located southeast of the castle on the same side of the river; its spires are easily visible from the castle. Built in 1172, the church is undergoing a great deal of remodeling to preserve much of its fine architecture, including a fifteenth-century carved oak choir stall and the stone carvings in one of the smaller chapels.

Limerick **Civic Center and City Hall** is right next to St. Mary's. It sits in stark contrast to the gray stone of the cathedral because it is in a modern building that is part of Limerick's riverfront facelift. It is of interest primarily in that it often houses special historic or contemporary exhibits. Check the local paper or at the civic center for more details.

From its small frontage on O'Connell Street you would not suspect that the **Belltable Arts Centre** houses an art gallery and theater. The gallery displays a variety of modern art. The theater company provides inexpensive plays by a variety of playwrights, including Shakespeare, and is certainly worth attending if you have an evening free. It is a very small theater with excellent performances. To get there, **follow O'Connell** toward the southwest part of the city. The arts center is on the block just after you cross the intersection with **Mallow Street**, just past **The Crescent** (a section of street that you'll recognize immediately by its shape).

German cyclists taking a pub break. An Irish pub lunch is filling fuel for the rest of the day's ride.

The **Limerick City Museum** is located on **St. John's Square** near **St. John's Cathedral**. (The cathedral is located several blocks due east of the tourist office mentioned above.) As city museums go this is a rather spacious building, and it displays a number of artifacts that were discovered at Lough Gur to the south. Relics of the siege of Limerick in the seventeenth century as well as letters and memorabilia from the Fenian rising of the 1860s are exhibited. Admission to the museum is free. Phone 417826 to check on current operating hours.

Monday, Thursday, and Saturday evenings offer **greyhound racing**. The stadium is on **Rossa Avenue** east of the city center. Follow **William Street**, and signs to Waterford, to the edge of town. Turn **left** a block after the fire station to get to the track.

DAYTRIP TO CRAGGAUNOWEN BRONZE AGE PROJECT (31 MILES ROUND TRIP)

Craggaunowen is a re-creation of a crannog, an area with farm dwellings built on a lake for protection from invaders during the fourth or fifth centuries. Right next to the lake is **Craggaunowen Castle**, which contains a number of medieval art specimens. Craggaunowen is only 15.5 miles from Limerick and is set in a picturesque, relatively unspoiled valley. There is an admission charge.

To get there leave Limerick from the **Sarsfield Bridge** and follow the Ennis/ Shannon Airport Road (**N18**). In 6 miles turn to the right toward Cratloe on **R462**. Four miles (10) of rolling terrain take you to the small town of Sixmilebridge. Continue straight for another 4 miles (14) following the signs for Craggaunowen Project. The last sign for the project points to the right and says "1 km," but it is more like another 1.5 miles (15.5). Entrance to the crannog is off to the left at the bottom of a hill. The shortest route back to Limerick is simply to retrace the way you came.

■■■■■■■■■■■■■■■■■■■■■■■■■■■■■■■■■■■■■■

TOUR 7
CORK TO KILLARNEY

Distance: 54.5 miles
Estimated time: 1–2 days
Terrain: Moderately hilly, especially in the latter half

This tour offers the chance to spend time both on and off your bike. You have the option of two splendid daytrips plus all of the attractions the city of Cork has to offer. Once you decide to leave Cork's busy atmosphere, your ride to Killarney traces the River Lee for many miles before taking you to a crossing of the Derrynasaggart Mountains.

CONNECTIONS. Cork is accessible by train from Tour 6 or you can fly there from either Shannon or Dublin airport. Cork is also easily reached by bus from Limerick.

CORK

"Oh, dear. You must be exhausted! Would you like some tea?" On two of my trips to Ireland I've heard words to this effect after disembarking at Cork Airport and making my way to my first night's lodging. Each time I had just finished recounting the ordeal of a long transatlantic flight and hours of waiting in airports. The words are typical of the warm welcome you receive in a city that truly seems to love visitors. And I can't think of any compelling reasons to disagree with Robert Gibbings, a poet and writer, who described Cork in this way: "Cork is the loveliest city in the world. Anybody who does not agree with me either was not born there or is prejudiced . . . . It is above all, a friendly city, one that you will not easily forget."

This city, which lends its name to the county it is in, lies in the southwest region of the country. It was founded by St. Finbarr in the late seventh century near where the River Lee empties into Cork Harbour. The Gaelic name for Cork, *Corcaigh*, means "marsh," which describes the ground when St. Finbarr arrived. First the Danes and then later, in the thirteenth century, the Normans settled nearby. The present arrangement of buildings in Cork is largely a result of Norman design. At one time a center of export of such products as butter and cattle, Cork proper is said to be somewhat a shadow of its former self. Still, there are dozens of remnants of Cork's medieval and seafaring past as well as modern shopping centers and thriving brewing and distilling companies.

Because of its size and its proximity to a large number of attractions, Cork is a good place to start a vacation, especially if you have limited time. Today some 180,000 people live in Cork, making it the second most populous city in the country. At times it seems as if most of them are trying to drive a vehicle

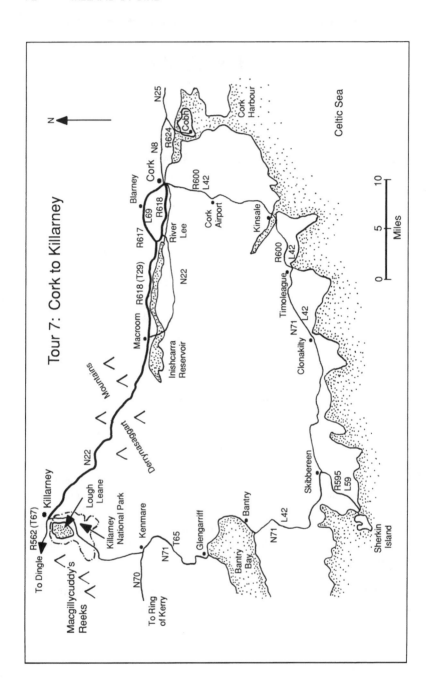

Tour 7: Cork to Killarney

into the narrow streets of the downtown. Those who aren't driving are walking, and there is constant jostling to try to keep from being spilled out into the road. As far as cycling goes, Cork is not soon to be on a list of "bicycle-friendly" cities. Because of the congested traffic and the large number of pedestrians, it is better to walk through downtown and leave your bike at your lodging.

The main streets follow the paths of waterways that were, up until the end of the eighteenth century, avenues of boat traffic. Indeed, early Cork must have resembled present-day Venice. Because the River Lee bisects and actually surrounds it, Cork is still very much a city of water. Sixteen bridges cross the river, connecting the city with the outlying areas. Two bridges built in the early to middle 1800s and one built in 1713 are still in use.

Cork is 4 miles north of the airport on **R600** (the Kinsale Road). The ride from the airport to town is completely (yes, completely) **downhill**. The main roads intersecting in or near Cork are **N71** from the south, **N22** from the west, **N20** from the north, and **N8** from the east.

Within downtown Cork the major north–south road is **Grand Parade** and the east–west one is **South Mall**. At the north end of Grand Parade, **Patrick Street** is the main thoroughfare leading east and north to the river. The *Bord Failte* office (phone 273251) lies at the corner of Grand Parade and South Mall. There are several good brochures available here to help you make the most of Cork. (Cork's telephone prefix is 021.)

The **post office** is found at the corner of **Pembroke Street** and **Oliver Plunkett Street**. From the *"i"* go east on **South Mall** to Pembroke, then **left** two blocks.

With such a wide variety of things to do and see in Cork, it is difficult to know where to begin. A good starting point might be the **Tourist Trail**, a walking tour of the city. A brochure of the trail is available at the *"i."* Starting from the **Grand Parade** right outside the tourist office, the trail winds its way through both the flat, modern (since 1750) city center and the old medieval city. Over thirty points of interest are described on this two- to three-hour walk that ends at **Camden Quay** on the north side of the river. You can also pick up the *Cork Guide*, which gives countywide descriptions and lots of historic data about the city.

Some of the interesting historic attractions along this path are **Parliament Bridge** and the nearby **Red Abbey**, which contains the remains of the oldest building in Cork. In 1690, a cannon was placed on top of the abbey tower to blast away at the eastern wall surrounding the city. The present-day **City Hall** is the site of an address President Kennedy gave while on his tour of Ireland. Evidence of the old waterways is apparent along the **South Mall**, where several eighteenth-century buildings have stone steps descending below the street to what was once the canal. Most popular of Cork's many churches is **St. Anne's**, otherwise called **Shandon Steeple** because of its location on Shandon Street.

This Protestant Church is renowned primarily for its "pepper-pot" top and for the chiming of its bells:

The bells of Shandon
That sound so grand
On the pleasant waters of the River Lee.

Built in 1720, the church was made famous in the 1830s by Francis Mahony (Father Prout) who wrote these lines in the poem "The Bells of Shandon." Strangely, the two sides of Shandon's edifice facing the city center are of cut white limestone and the two facing away are of red sandstone. Or as one verse puts it, "White and brown is Shandon's steeple, Parti-coloured like the people." One theory of why it was built this way holds that the white limestone was more expensive, so only the sides facing the city were done in it. The faces people were less likely to see were done in the cheaper sandstone.

As you approach the church you will likely be greeted by a variety of tunes being played on the famous chime of eight bells. That is because for a very small donation you can make the climb up into the steeple of the church and have a go at a tune or two. Laminated cards show you which ropes to pull and it's really quite fun. You can also climb a bit farther up where the bells actually are and then on to a parapet from which there is a good view of the entire city.

For another view of the city, make your way **south** from St. Anne's and turn left down **Dominick Street**. From **Widderling's Lane** you get a wonderful glimpse of the river and **St. Finbarr Cathedral** to the south of the city.

The **Crawford Municipal Art Gallery**, located just south of Lavitt's Quay on Emmet Place, houses works by modern Irish artists, and also houses a number of bronzes and sculptures. Right next door is Cork's **Opera House** (phone 270022), offering a potpourri of music, drama, and comedy.

If you're into sports, check the local papers to find out about upcoming hurling or Gaelic football matches. Even if you have never witnessed these before, just being part of an enthusiastic Irish crowd is worth the ticket price. You might even figure the game out by the time it's over. Another way to spend a sporty evening is at **Cork Greyhound Stadium** near the edge of town on **Western Road**. Racing is generally held on Monday, Wednesday, and Saturday nights.

For shopping, two markets worth checking out are the **City (English) Market** and the **Coal Quay Market**. City Market is an indoor maze of stalls offering fruits and vegetables, fresh meats, seafood, and a number of other commodities. Browse a while before you decide which stall has just the apple or banana you're looking for. City Market is found a couple of blocks north of the tourist office on the east side of Grand Parade.

The Coal Quay Market can be likened to a flea market. This outdoor hodgepodge of stalls, carts, and tables offers used books, fresh flowers, electronics, cassette tapes, used clothing, knickknacks, and various other items. Arrive during

A view from Shandon Steeple reveals one of Cork's tightly knit neighborhoods.

the week before 5:00 P.M. and you can immerse yourself in some hard bargaining. Coal Quay is just a few blocks north of City Market on Cornmarket Street.

Cork's major shopping district is on Patrick Street, where you can buy jewelry, Aran knitwear, pottery, clothing, artwork, and more. Of course, being on bike, if you buy something nice you'll have to have it shipped home. Waterford crystal tends not to last long in pannier bags.

DAYTRIP TO COBH (31 MILES ROUND TRIP)

A distance of 15.5 miles from town, a jaunt to Cobh, the "Cove of Cork," is a good way to spend the day. And summer is a good time to catch sailing races and regattas in Cork Harbour. Take **N8** east out of Cork. In about 3.5 miles **merge** to the **right** onto **N25**. N8 and N25 are very busy "dual carriageways" (four-lane highways) carrying traffic to Dublin and Rosslare. *Ride with extra care.* Most of the way on these two roads the shoulder is **fairly narrow** and rough. Be sure to have your tires properly inflated to avoid pinch flats. After another 5 miles (8.5) turn **right** on **R624**, which is welcome relief from the bustle of **N25**. Not long after making the turn, cross **Belvelley Bridge**. Beyond the bridge another 2 miles (10.5) is **Fota Wildlife Park**, a popular destination for both natives and tourists. It's more or less a zoo, but it also houses a wonderful arboretum, with plants from around the world. There's a small admission fee, and the hours are daily from 10:00 A.M. to 6:00 P.M. and Sunday from 11:00 A.M. to 6:00 P.M. Just a short distance from Fota, Cork Harbour becomes visible on your right, and you follow its shore most of the remaining 5 miles (15.5) to Cobh.

Cobh itself is a reasonably quiet seaside town with its complement of fishing vessels and sailboats. Cobh was often the point of departure for many Irish emigrants as they made their way to America. This was also the *Titanic's* last port of call before setting out on its ill-fated journey. Survivors of the *Lusitania*

The charming waterfront buildings of Cobh are dwarfed by the massive minarets of St. Colman's Cathedral.

were brought here after it was torpedoed off the coast in 1915. Directly down-town is a memorial to the victims.

The brick walkway along the waterfront is lined with benches, and after a stop at one of the several shops, this is a great spot for a snack or picnic lunch. The most noticeable structure in town is **St. Colman's Cathedral**, built in the mid-1860s. The forty-seven-bell carillon in its tower weighs 17.5 tons and is the largest in Ireland.

Public restrooms are on the harbor side of the main street at the entrance to John Fitzgerald Kennedy Memorial Park. Currently there is **no bike shop** in Cobh although asking around may help you find service.

DAYTRIP TO BLARNEY (9 MILES ROUND TRIP)

> *There is a stone there, that whoever kisses*
> *Oh, he never misses to grow eloquent.*
> *'Tis he may clamber to a lady's chamber*
> *Or become a member of Parliament.*

Father Prout penned these lines about the now famous stone at Blarney Castle. The castle, built in 1446 by Cormac MacCarthy, is not in perfect condi-tion, but crowds still flock to the site in order to kiss the stone and be given the gift of gab. Actually, to kiss the rock involves lowering yourself on your back onto a ledge, and an attendant holds your legs while you awkwardly kiss a worn stone in the wall. Despite the fact that tour busloads of people visit, and you'll likely have a wait, kissing the stone is really something you must do. The castle itself is a maze of dark, winding stairs that suddenly emerge into dim antecham-bers, the former bedrooms and dining halls of the castle's inhabitants.

The grounds surrounding the main building are magnificent. Several trails allow you to explore ancient haunts such as the Witches' Kitchen and the Wish-ing Steps. A host of primitive plants and ageless trees make this a botanist's dream. Perhaps the grounds are best described in this piece from an Irish poet:

> *The groves of Blarney, they are so charming*
> *Down by the purling of sweet silent streams,*
> *Being banked with posies that spontaneous grow there,*
> *Planted in order by the sweet rock close.*
> *'Tis there the daisy and the sweet carnation,*
> *The blooming pink and the rose so fair,*
> *The daffydowndilly, likewise the lily,*
> *All flowers that scent the sweet fragrant air.*

To get to Blarney from Cork sounds tricky but the way is well marked. Just keep your eyes on the passing tour buses and you'll be sure to find it. Go north on **Grand Parade** and turn **right** down **St. Patrick's**. Follow this across the bridge and take an **immediate left** on **Camden Quay**. Continue for a block or two until you veer to the **right** on **N20**, otherwise known as **John Street Upper**. Many side roads veer off **John Street**, so be careful to stay on the main road. This eventually becomes **Watercourse Road**. In about four blocks, take the fork to the **left** called **Commons Road**. You'll be on this road until you reach Blarney, about 4.5 miles away.

Besides Blarney Castle, another worthwhile stop in Blarney is **Blarney Woolen Mills**. Though not currently run by the original family, the mills have been around since 1824 producing knitwear of all sorts. In addition to the Blarney Castle Knitwear brand, you can buy Waterford and Cavan crystal, Aran handknits, and a large variety of other traditional Irish products. You can ship purchases home from here as well.

CORK TO MACROOM (24 MILES)

There are at least three good ways to get from Cork to Killarney. The southerly route follows the coastline. The northerly route cuts through the mountains. The central route, which follows the River Lee for several miles, is the most direct route and is the one described here.

Take **N22 west** out of Cork, which in 4 miles takes you to **R618** (**T29**) toward Blarney and Coachford. This road is considerably quieter than N22, and for the next 12 miles of rolling hills, the way passes through the Lee Valley with the River Lee just off to the south. At 13.5 miles from Cork is the small village of Dripsey. It's about here that you begin to feel you've left Cork city behind and have arrived in the countryside. Though it has little else to offer, Dripsey does have a pub and a public phone. Soon after passing the bridge outside of town there is a **monument**, inscribed in both English and Gaelic, to a battle fought between the English and Cork troops in 1921. This is marked by a **green arrow** sign on the roadside. After another 2.5 miles (16), as you pass through the slightly larger town of Coachford, there are **public restrooms** to the **right** at the edge of town.

For the next several miles there are occasional glimpses of the Inishcarra Reservoir, and the road is typically narrow and curvy. At 4.5 miles from Coachford (20.5), look to the right for a **narrow lane** where the main road used to go. There's an old **stone bridge** just off the lane, and since there's only a small amount of local traffic on it, the bridge is a good spot to relax if it happens to be lunch or snack time. Beyond this spot another 2.5 miles (23), the road intersects with **N22 west**, which continues the final mile to the town of Macroom.

If you don't plan to make the whole trip to Killarney in one day, Macroom is a decent spot for an overnight stay. At the very least, take time to dismount and have a look around. The main attraction in town is **Macroom Castle**, a fifteenth-century building that was once owned by Sir William Penn, a British admiral and father of the founder of Pennsylvania. Across the street from here is the daily farmer's market with the usual choice of fruits and vegetables. Just past the castle is a very nice walkway that follows the River Sullane as it cuts through town. Though it's not a big town, there are a number of pubs, restaurants, and B&Bs available.

MACROOM TO KILLARNEY (30.5 MILES)

To continue toward Killarney, pick up **N22** west again. You'll be passing through the **Derrynasaggart Mountains**, and there's only one main road through them from Macroom to Killarney. For 5.5 miles (28.5) the road is relatively wide and is fairly easy pedaling. In another 1.5 miles (30) the road **narrows** again and regains the close stone fences. In 4 miles (34) is Ballyvourney, a small crossroad town with a quilt shop, several souvenir places, a foodstore, and a couple of pubs. From here, the road gets considerably hillier and is **nearly all uphill** for 5 miles (39) to the **County Kerry** border. Though not marked as scenic on the map, this section of the ride from Macroom has an abundance of views of the River Sullane for the first 10 miles and then of the mountains the rest of the way.

Just as you enter Kerry there is a pulloff and a place to take in the surrounding mountains. You'll appreciate Kerry right from the start—the county sign is the beginning of a snaky, fast, 5-mile descent. At the base of the mountain (44), the road widens and the best shoulder between Cork and Killarney begins very shortly (recent, ongoing road work suggests that this shoulder may be extended). In 2.5 miles (46.5) there is a crossroad to the right marked for Mallow. Just beyond is a church. Across the road from the church is a petrol station/food shop. Water from the spigot on the site of the shop reportedly comes directly from the nearby mountains. If your water bottles are empty then this is the place to be. The remaining 8 miles into Killarney begin to pick up with **more traffic**; tour buses are especially common along here. The steep hill leading up to Killarney is a fitting end to an occasionally tough ride. Total distance to Killarney is 54.5 miles.

■ ■

TOUR 8
KILLARNEY TO WATERVILLE

Distance: 48 miles
Estimated time: 1–2 days
Terrain: Moderately hilly at the start, becoming very hilly.

The stretch of road from Killarney to Waterville contains some of the most popular sights in Ireland. Be prepared to ride neck and neck with tour buses as you approach some of the many scenic destinations. Though at times the riding is difficult, the vistas and seascapes are worth the effort.

CONNECTIONS. To get to Killarney by bike, follow the route described in Tour 7. Buses and trains also run to Killarney from Cork and Limerick. Flights are available from Shannon, Dublin, and Cork airports. The Killarney Airport is located 10 miles north of town on N23.

KILLARNEY

> *The splendor falls on castle walls*
> *And snowy summits old in story;*
> *The long light shakes across the lakes,*
> *And the wild cataract leaps in glory.*
> *Blow, bugle, blow, set the wild echoes flying.*
> *Blow, bugle; answer, echoes, dying, dying, dying.*

Thus wrote Alfred Lord Tennyson after his visit to the lakes of Killarney in 1848. This poem about the echoes of the boatman's bugle over the water is said to have spurred an increase in the tourist trade after its publication.

Killarney (in Irish, *Cill Airne*, "the Church of the Sloes") is one of Ireland's most visited destinations. Lord Kenmare was responsible for establishment of the town in the early 1750s. He began the tourist business and instigated the building of major roads leading out in all directions. Though Killarney has only a fraction of the population of Cork, around 10,000, the Killarney surroundings are a major attraction. In fact, Killarney can handle over 6,000 visitors at any one time. This seems quite a feat for such a small town until you ride down Muckross Road with its line of B&Bs and the fairly new hotels that have been constructed.

Despite the fact that you're likely to be passed by a number of buses carrying hordes of sightseers, the crowds seem manageable and Killarney still has a mostly small-town atmosphere. No doubt, drivers will try to persuade you to take their horsedrawn jaunting carts, and hundreds of small signs try to entice you with "Music Nightly," "Lunch Specials," or "Bike Hire Available," but

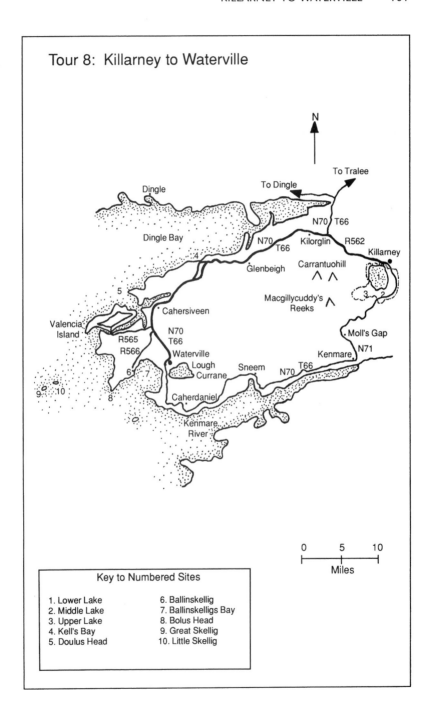

Tour 8: Killarney to Waterville

Key to Numbered Sites

1. Lower Lake
2. Middle Lake
3. Upper Lake
4. Kell's Bay
5. Doulus Head
6. Ballinskellig
7. Ballinskelligs Bay
8. Bolus Head
9. Great Skellig
10. Little Skellig

Killarney is far from the American version of a tourist trap. Prices tend to be somewhat higher because of the town's popularity, but there are a number of pubs, restaurants, and accommodations with moderate prices. There are at least three hostels in town. Killarney's telephone prefix is 064.

The *Bord Failte* office (phone 31633) is on **Main Street** (Main Street becomes High Street and then Rock Road as you travel north, or Muckross Road as you travel to the south). If you're coming in from Macroom, stay on that road and follow the signs to the town center. This road is **East Avenue Road** and passes the **Court House** and **St. Mary's Church**. On the west side of the street, across from the church is the *"i."*

There are at least three **bike shops** in Killarney and a number of bike rental places as well. You should have little trouble finding parts or having repairs done.

Because of its size compared to Cork, Killarney proper has considerably less to see and do. It's not Killarney itself that attracts the great number of tourists, but the nearby lake district. However, there are a few things in town worth taking time to see. An excellent map is the **Killarney Area Guide**. On one side the map shows the nearby lakes, topography, points of interest, and the roads that lead to them. On the other side is historical information, a list of entertainment choices, nature trails, and a Killarney city map. **The Kerry Guide** gives additional information about the Killarney area as well as the rest of County Kerry.

St. Mary's Cathedral (not to be confused with St. Mary's Church) is an example of the neo-Gothic style that was built in the mid-1840s. The nineteenth-century architect Pugin designed the cross-shaped limestone structure that took nearly ten years to build. To find the cathedral follow **New Street west** until it intersects **Port Road** from the north. St. Mary's is on the right. A **Poet's Monument** is located toward the east of town on College Street past the Court House, across from the **Franciscan Friary**. Known as *Speir Bhean*, which means "Beautiful Woman," the sculpture by Seamus Murphy was set up in the 1940s to recognize County Kerry's Gaelic-speaking poets. The friary dates to 1860 and is similar in style to Muckross Abbey, which is near the lakes.

July and August are excellent times to catch **boat races** or attend boating carnivals on the lakes. Check a calendar of events for specific times and dates. **Gaelic football** and **hurling** are regular Sunday events as well. The local paper will give more information.

There's no shortage of places to shop in Killarney for souvenirs. Jewelry, clothes, wool products, crystal, and any number of other products are available in the numerous downtown shops.

DAYTRIP TO THE LAKES OF KILLARNEY (8 MILES ROUND TRIP)

As mentioned earlier, Killarney's strongest appeal is the lake district with its three famous lakes: Upper, Middle, and Lower. These terms are essentially

Ireland's rainy climate produces an abundance of spectacular waterfalls. This one is Torc Waterfall in Killarney National Park. Photo by Jeff Kirchhoff

opposites since **Lower Lake (Lough Leane)** is farthest north and **Upper Lake** is to the south. Lough Leane is also largest of the three with **Middle** or **Muckross Lake** next in size. The lakes are nestled at the base of **Macgillycuddy's Reeks**, a mountain range that includes Ireland's highest peak, **Carrantuohill** (3,414 feet). All are in **Killarney National Park**. Though definitely not considered tall by most measures, the mountains are only the weathered remains of much higher terrain formed 400 million years ago. The same glacial forces that carved away

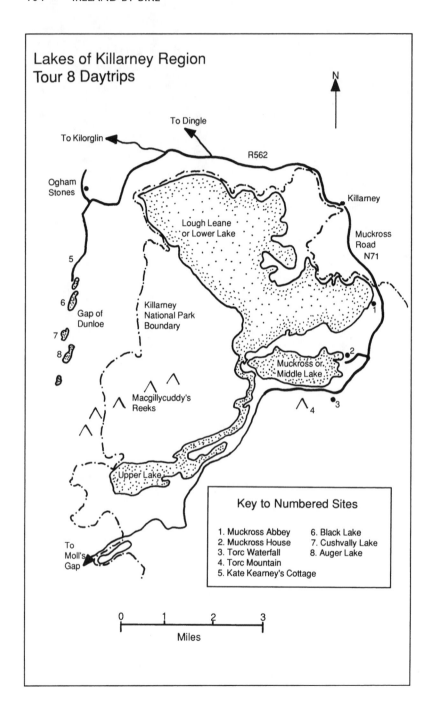

Lakes of Killarney Region
Tour 8 Daytrips

N

To Dingle

To Kilorglin

R562

Ogham
Stones

Killarney

Lough Leane
or Lower Lake

Muckross
Road
N71

5

6

Gap of
Dunloe

Killarney
National Park
Boundary

1

7

8

2

Muckross or
Middle Lake

3

Macgillycuddy's
Reeks

4

Upper Lake

Key to Numbered Sites

1. Muckross Abbey   6. Black Lake
2. Muckross House   7. Cushvally Lake
3. Torc Waterfall   8. Auger Lake
4. Torc Mountain
5. Kate Kearney's Cottage

To
Moll's
Gap

0   1   2   3

Miles

the mountains also contributed to the forming of the lakes. Killarney and the lakes are the easternmost part of the Iveragh Peninsula, which thrusts itself out into the Atlantic. To the north it is bordered by Dingle Bay, to the south by the Kenmare River.

Cycling south on the Muckross Road (**N71**) takes you to a bike/jaunting car path off to the right that parallels the busy road. The path begins about a mile from the edge of Killarney. In less than a mile from its start the path turns and enters **Killarney National Park** and onto a smaller trail. Follow this to the fifteenth-century **Muckross Abbey**, founded for a group of Franciscan monks by Donal McCarthy, Chieftain of Desmond. As is true of most of the ancient Irish ruins, you're free to walk around, climb up, and explore. Though the roof is missing, many of the portals, windows, and arches are still intact. A cemetery that contains both very old and fairly recent headstones surrounds the abbey.

From the abbey follow the signs again toward **Muckross House**. At the fork follow the route marked to the Cottage rather than to Muckross (if you have a couple of hours to spare). This path runs about 4.5 miles around the lakes, for much of the way following the shoreline of Lough Leane. It is a very beautiful ride and well worth doing if time permits. The trail eventually leads back to the main road. Turn left (north) onto this. In another mile and a half or so is the turnoff and carpark for **Torc Waterfall**, which is one of the finest in Ireland. The trail leading to the waterfall is for hiking only so park your bike near the interpretive center at the base. Beyond the waterfall the trail continues to climb and there are some fabulous views of the lakes region.

Continuing north on the road from the waterfall takes you back to Muckross House where you can lock your bike on a rail while you tour. This nineteenth-century manor has been extensively refurnished with period pieces and sits amid sculptured hedges and a flowered landscape. From the ground floor windows there is also a terrific view of Middle Lake. The ivy-covered mansion has an extensive museum that features aspects of Kerry folklife. The craft center in the basement includes a working forge and printing press, as well as numerous other pieces of equipment. There is an admission charge to tour the house.

DAYTRIP TO THE GAP OF DUNLOE (16 MILES ROUND TRIP)

Another worthwhile trip is a ride out to explore the Gap of Dunloe. Though magnificent anytime, the Gap is truly splendid in the late morning; the fog is burning off, the sun is peeking through, and the air is fresh and still. Later in the day the crowds increase and some of the valley's charm is lost to the bustle of the tourists.

To get there take **New Street west** out of town. This veers north (right) at St. Mary's Cathedral and the National Park entrance. Up ahead, the road goes **left** to Kilorglin and the Ring of Kerry. This is **R562**. In 3.5 miles take the

A lonely round tower draws cyclists down one of many quiet backroads.

marked road left to the Gap of Dunloe. The turn is about **three hundred yards** past the **Hotel Europe**. In another 2.5 miles (6) you arrive at a sharp left hand bend in the road near the **Dunloe Castle Hotel**. Instead of turning at this point, go straight past the hotel down the hill. At the bottom of the hill turn **right** and go up the hill (total of 0.5 mile from the hotel) to some excellent examples of **Ogham stones**. These are slender stones scratched with an ancient form of writing. They date from the late Iron Age, around A.D. 300, and are marked with a series of diagonal or horizontal lines. The writing is read from the bottom upward, and these stones are supposedly inscribed with the names of deceased persons and their families.

Pedal back up to the hotel and turn **right** to the Gap, which is just a little over a mile away (8). **Kate Kearney's Cottage** is at the entrance. You'll find food and souvenirs here, and if you have extra money you can hire a carriage and pony to take you through. Although the trail is a bit rough at times, most bikes can also make the trip; otherwise hiking is probably the best way. Carry some water and food with you if you plan to hike for awhile; there are very few services along the way and you will most likely return the same way you came.

Regardless of how you get there, the valley, which was created from glacial meltwater, is stunning. There are numerous exposed rock outcroppings, and sheep graze in the lower areas among the ferns. Streams and tiny rivulets coming off the mountains seem everpresent; water literally permeates the valley. The trail takes you by five small lakes, the second of which is **Black Lake**, where one legend has it that St. Patrick drowned the last snake.

THE RING OF KERRY

The Ring of Kerry is a circular route around the biggest part of the Iveragh Peninsula. It is a part of Ireland that easily wears two faces. It's a popular tourist spot and **loads of tourist buses and rental cars** are bound to pass you by, especially in July and August. To serve those tourists there are dozens of "tourist centres" offering "traditional" gifts and souvenirs while essentially commercializing the whole affair.

On the other hand, because the distance around the Ring is fairly long, over 100 miles, the crowds don't tend to congregate in any one spot. Because the route is circuitous, there are of course two directions you could go to cover it, but the counterclockwise one is most often recommended and that is the one described here. Supposedly there is less traffic in this direction but I don't really think it matters. In this tour, approximately half of the Ring, from Killarney to Waterville, is described. The stretch from Waterville back to Killarney is recounted in the next tour. The entire ring can take anywhere from two to four days, depending on the number of stops and how fast you tackle the plentiful hills.

KILLARNEY TO KILORGLIN (12 MILES)

Follow **New Street west** out of Killarney until it turns left to Kilorglin and becomes **R562**. The first 3.5 miles are the same as the route taken to the Gap of Dunloe. The next 8.5 miles are the least scenic part of the trip because the high fences and overgrowth keep you from looking off into the distance, while the passing buses force you to keep your eyes on the road. One consolation is that it's flat. As you enter Kilorglin (12), follow the road as it winds its way **up the hill**. It is lined with dozens of shops and is quite a busy place. There are a number of pubs, cafés, and B&B accommodations here.

In August, Kilorglin holds its annual cattle and sheep fair called **Puck Fair**. The name comes from King Puck, a wild goat that is captured and made king of the three-day celebration. To continue, follow the road to Cahersiveen, which takes a left at the top of the hill.

KILORGLIN TO CAHERSIVEEN (26 MILES)

Kilorglin to Glenbeigh is a distance of 8.5 miles, and for a shorter ride this is a good stopping point. There are several B&Bs both outside of and within Glenbeigh (20.5). There is a campground located about 0.5 mile into town on the right. Though there is **no bike shop** you may be able to get minor repairs done at the **Shell** station in the town center. There is also **camping** just through the town and past the stone towers on the left. The towers were built in the 1870s, and there is a good view of several mountain lakes from them.

After Glenbeigh the road becomes **much hillier**. A mile-long ascent (22) brings you to the crest of a hill with your first good look at the sea from the Ring. The following mile-long descent (23) hugs the coast as the road outlines Dingle Bay. After this descent, you begin to travel in the Kerry of rich green pastures bordered by brilliant blue sea. In 5 miles (28), there is a highly recommended **detour** off the main road following the lane to **Kells Bay** to the **right**. Be warned that this is a 2-mile descent and you'll eventually have to come back up, though not by exactly the same route.

As you descend, turn **right** at the "Strand" (beach) sign. At the bottom is a

A "mad sunny" day inspires a cyclist to shed the rain gear and catch some rays on a lunch break.

beach, pier, and campground. If the weather cooperates you may choose to join the Irish for a swim in the chilly waters. There is also a B&B, restaurant, foodstore, and public toilet. From the strand you can get a clear view of the Dingle Peninsula, which you may be riding in Tour 10.

A worthwhile excursion to take from Kells Bay either on foot or by mountain bike is the tiny "boreen" (lane) to the right marked simply "Roads." Though eventually this dead-ends, it continues for about 2 miles along the mountainside. On this deserted stretch of mountain road you can't help but feel the magic of the land with the fresh air blowing from the bay and the stone fences cropping up all around you on the steep slopes. If you look far off across the bay you can see the outer edge of Dingle Harbour with the tiny white buildings perched on its shores. To get back to the main road from the strand, go back up the way you came down. Go **right** at the crossroads and then left at the sign for **Kells Post Office**. The post office, not counting the Kells Bay detour, is 30 miles from Killarney.

From the Kells Post Office to Cahersiveen is 8 miles (38), and the road, because it angles away from the bay, is slightly less scenic than the preceding section. Cahersiveen has a number of B&B accommodations, a hostel, plenty of places to get groceries, and of course, pubs. The town claims to be the hub of the Iveragh Peninsula, but Cahersiveen is very quaint and quiet compared to the commotion of Kilorglin and other towns closer to Killarney. Perhaps its charm lies in the smell of burning peat, which seems to pervade the air, giving the town a warm, welcoming feel. Or it could be the narrow streets with the occasional sidewalk vendor selling fresh fruit.

Whatever it is that attracts one to Cahersiveen, this is also a good place to spend the night, especially for middle-distance riders. Various pubs in town host traditional singing at night. Near the monument to the soldiers of the Easter Rebellion you'll find a tourist information point displaying a map of Cahersiveen and interesting facts about the Ring of Kerry. Just before the statue of the Fenian soldier is a road to the right leading to a popular swimming beach at White Strand. The town's bike shop is at the west end of town on the right.

CAHERSIVEEN TO WATERVILLE (10 MILES)

On leaving Cahersiveen simply stay on the main road out of town and follow the signs. Much of the way is through relatively flat, boggy terrain. There are several locations along the way where turf is frequently cut from the bog. The air can be heavy with the rich smell of the peat burning in nearby homes, which adds to the flavor (literally) of the ride. From Cahersiveen 8.5 miles (46.5) is a **campground** and 1.5 miles farther (48) at the entrance to Waterville is another.

Waterville (*An Coireán*, meaning "little whirlpool") is a neatly kept, friendly town perched right on the lip of **Ballinskelligs Bay**. From the public carpark, look out to the right at Bolus Head and to the left at Hog's Head. The breeze from the bay is refreshing, and it blows away the peat smoke that had settled back in the boglands. Waterville has a singular, mystical history that claims the first Celtic invaders, from whom the Gaelic nation descended, landed here in Ballinskelligs Bay in 1700 B.C. A few remains of this legendary invasion are described in the next tour as it leaves Waterville.

Near the carpark are public toilets, and there is a variety of foodstores and pubs to provide needed refueling. There are plenty of places to sleep for the night including B&Bs and a hostel. There is a **bike shop** near the edge of town right before going over the bridge.

■ ■

TOUR 9

WATERVILLE TO KILLARNEY

Distance: 51 miles
Estimated time: 1–2 days
Terrain: Very hilly at times, with stretches of more moderate climbing

This tour continues along the verdant coastal scenery in the previous tour. Along the way are sites of historical significance, especially the former home of Daniel O'Connell in Derrynane. The last several miles of the trip take you away from the coast and back into the mountains of Killarney National Park.

CONNECTIONS. Buses from both Cork and Killarney service Waterville. To reach Waterville by bike, follow the route described in Tour 8.

WATERVILLE TO SNEEM (23 MILES)

This section describes the second half of the Ring of Kerry tour begun in Tour 8. The scenery in this section is every bit as striking as that in the first half, if not more so. There is notably **more climbing** in this part of the tour because of the number of miles of jagged coastline the road follows.

Leave Waterville **south** on N70. A mile from the edge of town look to the left to see **Eightercua**, four stones aligned on a hilltop. This is supposedly where the wife of an ancient invader is buried. From Eightercua the road ascends up to **Coomakista Pass** where there are some splendid panoramic views. On the way up, stop at the **church** and walk around back to get a glimpse back at Waterville far below and Ballinskelligs Bay to the west. At the carpark at the top, several islands are spread out before you and the rugged cliffs of **Sheehan's Point** are at your feet. To the right are **Scariff Island** and **Deenish Island**. Directly in front are **The Bull**, **The Cow**, and **The Calf** (from right to left). These mark the mouth of the Kenmare River. This point is 4 miles (4) from the center of Waterville. From here the harbor of Derrynane and its strands are also visible far to the left. Historically this was an important point of trade with countries such as France and Spain.

Descend 2.5 miles (6.5) from the Coomakista viewpoint and turn **right** on the road to Derrynane. Another narrow, winding descent of 1 mile (7.5) brings you to a crossroad. To the right are the strand and pier; to the left is Derrynane House. The house and wooded grounds on which it sits belonged to Daniel O'Connell and his ancestors but is now a national monument and park. A garden walk takes you among some lovely exotic plants, and the house and interpretive center are worth a visit. There is a small admission charge, and the hours are weekdays 9:00 A.M. to 6:00 P.M. and Sunday 11:00 A.M. to 7:00 P.M.

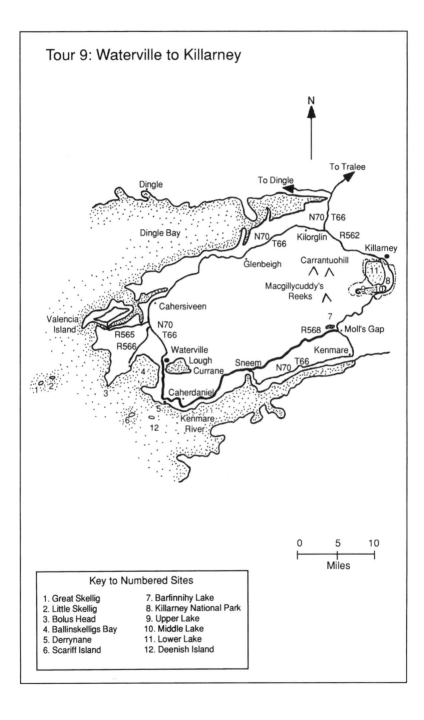

Tour 9: Waterville to Killarney

N

To Tralee

To Dingle

Dingle

Dingle Bay

N70 / T66

Glenbeigh

N70

T66

Kilorglin

R562

Killarney

Carrantuohill

Macgillycuddy's
Reeks

11

8

9

10

Cahersiveen

Valencia
Island

N70

T66

7

R568

Moll's Gap

R565

R566

Waterville

Lough
Currane

Kenmare

Sneem

N70 / T66

4

Caherdaniel

5

6

12

Kenmare
River

0   5   10
Miles

Key to Numbered Sites

1. Great Skellig
2. Little Skellig
3. Bolus Head
4. Ballinskelligs Bay
5. Derrynane
6. Scariff Island
7. Barfinnihy Lake
8. Killarney National Park
9. Upper Lake
10. Middle Lake
11. Lower Lake
12. Deenish Island

Dense foliage and a stone arch accent a church near Sneem, a crossroads village on the Ring of Kerry. Photo by Jeff Kirchhoff

From Derrynane take the road marked to Caherdaniel rather than back-tracking to the original turnoff. It's 1.5 miles (9) to Caherdaniel where there's a hostel, B&B, and post office. Right outside of town is the old stone caher, or fort, that gives the town its name. This town at one time provided the copper ore that was traded with Spain out of Derrynane Harbor, but there's little left here now. Beyond Caherdaniel 1 mile (10) on the right is a campground.

As you leave town, the next several miles provide a substantially different landscape. The cliffs are replaced by sweeping views of the 3-mile-wide **Kenmare River** across boulder-strewn terrain. In 3 miles (13) is the town hamlet of Westcove and 0.5 mile beyond that is Castlecove. Expect to find few services at either location. From Caherdaniel 8 miles (18) you ascend for awhile and the road turns away from the river. As you reach the **top of the pass** there is a re-markable view of the Sneem Valley to the north. From this vantage several peaks, namely **Knocknagantee**, **Mullaghanattin**, and **Carrantuohill**, are just visible in the distance. Just under 5 miles (23) from the summit is Sneem.

SNEEM TO KILLARNEY (28 MILES)

This is one of the most exciting little towns on the entire Ring. What Cahersiveen has in quiet charm, Sneem has in ardor and enthusiasm. There is a carnival-like atmosphere, and the street just beyond the bridge is busy with tourists. People seem to be milling about everywhere. Sneem has a **bike shop**, several B&Bs, plenty of reasonably priced gift shops, a museum, pubs, and restaurants. This is definitely a good stopping point if you don't relish additional miles right away.

To ride on toward Killarney take the **first left** after the bridge on **R568**. From Sneem the road gradually ascends for 5.5 miles (28.5), and then there is an easy descent for 2.5 miles (31) through more boulder-covered land. After only a mile or so of relatively level terrain, the road generally ascends for the next 5 miles (37) to **Barfinnihy Lake**. The climbing along this route from Sneem is sometimes challenging, but a major consolation is the seeming lack of tour buses most of the way. Once you get to **Moll's Gap** in another 0.5 mile (37.5) and take the crossroad **left** to Killarney, the odds of seeing tour buses go up again. The climb to Moll's Gap is not without merit. There is a rewarding view of the **Black Valley** all around and the mountains of Killarney National Park loom plainly visible ahead.

A daunting climb at times, 3 more miles (40.5) take you to the southern-most boundary of the park where there's a **carpark** off to the left. This is perhaps the best place from which to see the Killarney Valley with Carrantuohill rising in the distance and Upper Lake to the north. You'll also find a map showing the names and features of the lakes, valleys, and mountains. Down the mountain another 0.5 mile (41) is a viewing point called **Ladies View**, reportedly so named because of the infatuation Queen Victoria's ladies-in-waiting had for this spot. The view from here is nice, but it is less spectacular than that from the entrance sign back up the road. From this viewpoint the road snakes its way downhill for 6 miles (47) until you find yourself at the entrance to Torc Waterfall to the right. From here it is another 4 miles to Killarney, making the total just over 51 miles.

■ ■

TOUR 10
KILLARNEY TO DINGLE

Distance: 41 miles
Estimated time: 1 day
Terrain: Moderate to hilly, particularly toward the end

Traveling mostly northwest out of Killarney, the first third of this ride is primarily through easy-to-pedal farmland. When you turn west the road becomes hillier and the views more fantastic. The winds and sands of Dingle Bay are constant companions for the latter half of this trip.

CONNECTIONS. If you are following the outline of tours in this book, you can reach Killarney by bike via Tour 9. Buses and trains also run to Killarney from Cork and Limerick. Flights are available from Shannon, Dublin, and Cork airports. The Killarney Airport is located 10 miles north of town on N23.

KILLARNEY TO INCH (25.5 MILES)
Follow **R562** (**T67**) **west** out of Killarney just as if you were going to the Ring of Kerry. In 3 miles turn **right** on **R563** at the town of Fossa toward Milltown. In a short distance you pass the IYH hostel, **Aghadoe House**. This road is steep at times and is a good stretch of the legs after leaving Killarney. There is little of the boulder-covered landscape for which the Ring of Kerry and the Gap of Dunloe are known. Instead, you ride through more heather, wildflowers, and hay pastures than anything else. This is definitely off the beaten path and most of the vehicles appear to be local with only an occasional tour bus; most of the traffic takes the main road out of Killarney to Tralee. Nine miles (12) from the **R563** turnoff is Milltown. There are a couple of B&Bs, pubs, and a public phone. At the end of town go **right** on **N70** toward Tralee.

Down the road 1.5 miles (13.5), take the **left** turn to Castlemaine, which is only 0.5 mile (14) beyond. There are pubs, a phone, and a foodstore here, as well as a couple of B&Bs. Just over the bridge at the town crossroads go **left** at the sign to Dingle on **R561**. Beyond town 3.5 miles (17.5), look to the left to see the first good view of Castlemaine Harbour. From here the road begins to parallel the harbor for several miles. In 2 more miles (19.5) a post office sits on the right. The next 6 miles to Inch (25.5) the road gradually works its way uphill. In Inch there are B&Bs, a hostel, a pub, and a restaurant.

INCH TO DINGLE (15.5 MILES)
Just down the road 1 mile (26.5) is **Inch Strand**. If the sun peeks through, the waters of the harbor are brilliant and stand in contrast to the rich green of the pastures on one side and the smoky-colored mountains on the other. If

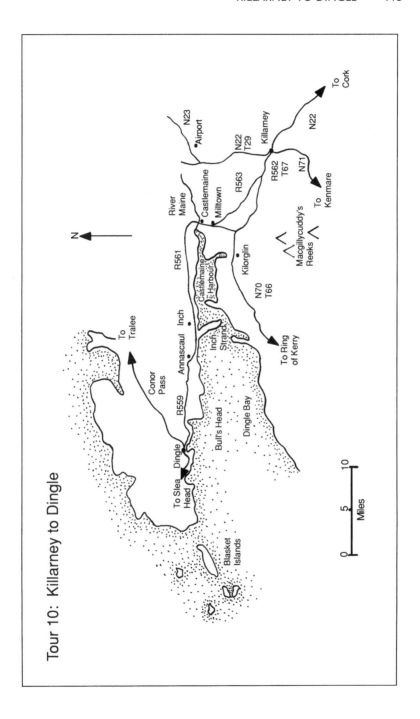

Tour 10: Killarney to Dingle

you've some time to spare, the strand is a nice place to spend some of it. Irish families find this a wonderful place for holiday, and the name Inch really understates the long stretch of sand available. There are wildly sculptured rocks and miles of sand. This is a good safe place to go wading if you can brave the cool air and cooler water. The Irish children playing barefoot with their sand buckets are probably enough to convince you that it can't be *that* cold. About a mile along the strand in a big break in the dunes are traces of the sandhill dwellers who lived here as long ago as the Iron Age and maybe earlier.

The road from Inch follows the coast for 4 miles (30.5) with sweeping vistas of the harbor and the strand. Beware of the acute bends as you fly down some of the descents. After 0.5 mile (31.5) from where the road turns away from the coast you'll reach a sign pointing right to Annascaul, which has some B&Bs, camping, and a hostel. To continue to Dingle take the **left fork** at the Annascaul signpost. The road is now **R559**. The next 7 miles (38.5) are mostly a narrow, winding ascent through the sheep and cow pastures so common in this area. A mist and fog commonly roll in from the sea and flavor the land with a taste not quite heavy enough to call rain, but just enough to get the water dripping off your helmet. In another 1.5 miles (40) you crest the final hill of the journey to Dingle. You'll know you're to this point when you come upon the numerous signs advertising Dingle hotels. Take an opportunity to look out over the harbor from here, then enjoy the easy coast the rest of the way into town. Off to the right as you coast down the hill is the entrance to an excellent hostel. Total trip distance from Killarney to Dingle is 41 miles.

DINGLE

The town of Dingle lies near the western edge of the peninsula that bears its name. The peninsula, known in Irish as *Corca Dhuibhne* (pronounced *corka gweena*), or "Seed of the Goddess," is a finger of land that stretches out nearly 30 miles into the Atlantic Ocean. The western fringe of the peninsula is dotted with a number of historically important islands, including the famous Blasket Islands.

Dingle itself dates back to pre-medieval times, and at one time was County Kerry's primary harbor. Today it is certainly not a bustling seaport; it would be more accurate to describe it as a quiet fishing village that is annually invaded by a large number of foreigners. Several things draw visitors to this western outpost, not least of which is its ideal location as a base for exploring the rest of the peninsula. But that is not the only reason for coming here.

While Dingle has managed to escape some of the excessive numbers that are attracted to Killarney and the Ring of Kerry, tourism is still its major industry. During the high season, the tourists far outnumber the locals. But it does seem to have been able to absorb the influx without a loss of its character and heritage and it is still a fun, truly Irish town.

The trawlers still pass in and out of Dingle Harbour, much as they have for countless generations. And despite the tourists, many of the shops close early as the natives head home to snug themselves against the chilly Atlantic breeze or make their way to a pub for a round of stout. Perhaps the most remarkable thing about the town is the close ties it has with the land. Nearby pastures are dotted with sheep, and hay is still cut from pastures that have been producing rich grass for centuries for Dingle farmers. Not many places in Ireland manage to capture the sea-and-stone romance quite the way that Dingle does.

The main road coming into Dingle from the east becomes a one-way going the opposite direction as soon as you hit town. When you come to this point turn **right** toward Conor Pass. This is **The Mall** and leads to John Street. A **left** on **John Street** takes you a half block to the "*i,*" which is in a small office on the left. John Street becomes **Main** and then **Upper Main** as you travel west

Ogham stones, etched with writings of the past, are reminders of ancient days.

on it. The post office, two banks, and several shops and restaurants are on Main, just up the hill from the "*i.*" **Dykegate Street** and **Green Street** are the two primary roads that connect Main back to the harbor road to the south.

The majority of the pubs and a number of shops are on the street called **The Wood** or **Strand Street**, which runs along the harbor and pier.

Besides the tourist office, another good spot for Irish literature and sightseeing information is *An Cafe Liteartha*. This combination bookshop and café contains an assortment of reading material that is mostly of Irish origin or about the Irish. In back of the bookstore is a small restaurant that serves sandwiches, pastries, breads, and tea. It's a nice quiet place to go to pore over your guidebooks or to talk over your plans with the other cyclists or hikers who tend to frequent the place.

Dingle is a perfect size for exploration by foot. Walk out on the pier to watch the fishing boats return from a day of work. From here you can also see

The author explores a beehive hut near Dingle and realizes that earlier inhabitants were a bit shorter. Photo by Jeff Kirchhoff

the lay of the town, its houses scattered along the harbor. Tucked between the sea and the mountains, Dingle occupies the only flat ground around. Near the pier there are a number of shops where you can find a variety of both traditional and contemporary crafts.

For a more guided tour of the area pick up Maurice Sheehy's book, *A Motorist's Guide to the Dingle Peninsula*, which, despite its name, describes several walking tours of Dingle and locales nearby. Especially good is the walk toward the east of town along the coast. The trail takes you by a **stone tower** built in the 1840s as part of a famine-relief work project. Beyond the tower is a **lighthouse** built in 1886 and lit by kerosene for nearly one hundred years until it was converted to electricity. Just before the lighthouse is a path through the fence down to a sea cave said to have been a hideout for Marie Antoinette.

Though Dingle is small, the town swells in population considerably during the summer months. This explains why there are fifty pubs (unofficially) in this town of 1,500. At a ratio of only thirty people per pub, this must be one of the highest densities of pubs anywhere on the island. And it certainly gives a visitor no excuse for staying home at night. A walk down the main streets uncovers dozens of possibilities for traditional music, seafood, and pints.

Since the late 1980s Dingle has also been home to the famous **dolphin**, Fungi, who resides in Dingle Harbour. Assuming that Fungi is still alive by the time you travel to Ireland, boat excursions leave the pier on a regular basis to take tourists to see, photograph, and even swim with him. Gift shops carry his picture on everything from coffee mugs to posters, and he is the unofficial symbol of the town.

Another fun stop, especially if you have children with you, is **Oceanworld**, a relative newcomer to Dingle's line of attractions. The aquaria and tanks set up throughout the building house sea creatures from a number of different habitats found in the country. There is also a petting tank where you can stick your hand in to rub the belly of a ray or flounder, and the attendants from time to time pull out crabs, starfish, and other sea creatures for kids to hold. There is an admission charge and family rates are offered. Oceanworld is open from 10:00 A.M. daily (phone 066 52111).

DAYTRIP TO SLEA HEAD (29.5 MILES ROUND TRIP)

As in Killarney, many of Dingle's features lie outside of town and within relatively short cycling distance. A perfect day of touring goes around **Slea Head**, the tip of the peninsula. In fact, this is one of the most inspiring trips in the whole of Ireland. You may find yourself passing and being passed by the same cyclists, cars, and certainly buses on the entire circuit. There's a new picture around every corner, and it's difficult to keep up any kind of pace with so many opportunities to stop.

At 0.5 mile west of Dingle Pier take a **left** over the bridge to Slea Head. In 2.5 miles (3) there is a **campground** beyond the signs for Ballymore House. Up the road a bit from here is a good view of **Ventry Harbour**. Ventry is the site of a legendary third-century battle between Fionn MacCumhail and the King of the World (Daire Doon). It was on the beach here that Fionn killed the King of the World and many of his troops. At the far side of Ventry (4.5) is a hostel.

In 3.5 miles (8) look to the left for Dunbeg, a promontory stone fort perched on a high cliff overlooking the Atlantic. To the right is a carpark and a good place to lean your bike. Though not large by most standards, the two thousand-year-old fort has several interesting features. A *clochaun*, or **beehive hut**, stands near one of the walkways inside the fort. Beehive huts are structures

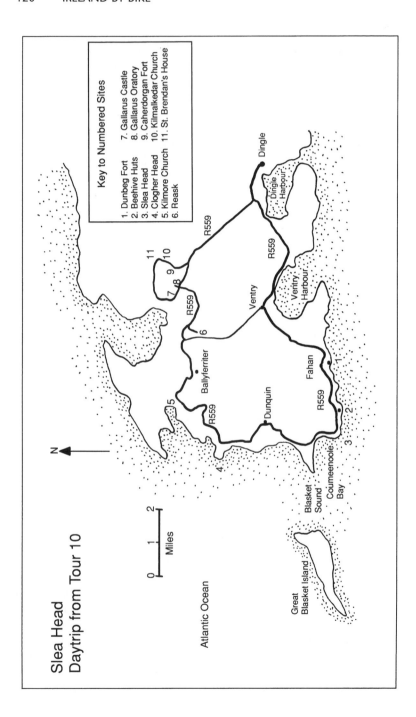

Slea Head
Daytrip from Tour 10

Key to Numbered Sites

1. Dunbeg Fort
2. Beehive Huts
3. Slea Head
4. Clogher Head
5. Kilmore Church
6. Reask
7. Gallarus Castle
8. Gallarus Oratory
9. Caherdorgan Fort
10. Kilmalkedar Church
11. St. Brendan's House

made of piled stones that get their name from their oblong shape. This one is reconstructed well enough that visitors can climb inside. Perhaps the most astonishing thing about Dunbeg is the rate at which it is being lost to the erosive forces of the Atlantic. When built, the outer wall of the fort must have been dozens of yards from the cliff's edge, but over the centuries over half of the fort has fallen into the sea. It will only be a matter of time before the whole structure is lost. There is a small admission charge to tour the area.

Just under 1 mile (9) from here there are several places to view additional beehive huts. They are on private land, and the owners charge a small fee to walk up to see them. One of the best is **Caher Murphy**, which contains several mostly roofless huts. In another 1.5 miles (10.5) is the white **Calvary Cross**, which indicates that you are at Slea Head. There is a pulloff with a terrific view of the **Blasket Islands** to the west across Blasket Sound. The nearest and largest of the islands is **Great Blasket**, essentially uninhabited since the islanders were relocated to the mainland in the early 1950s. The islands have been the subject of many books, several of which were written by native Blasket Islanders (see "Language and Literature" in Part I for recommended reading).

A mile farther (11.5) is a carpark. From here you can see the strand and the road leading down to it. At the next crossroad the left fork takes you to the strand

Gallarus Oratory, on the Dingle Peninsula, is a watertight twelfth-century stone church built completely without mortar.

Seventh-century carvings on stone obelisks near Reask, County Kerry. Photo by Jeff Kirchhoff

while the right continues the path around Slea Head. Beyond the crossroad are several places where the road has been moved inland, a reminder of how fast erosion is taking place along the coast. In 1 mile (12.5) the road turns left at the sign for "Ferry." Having read the books about the Blaskets and now having seen them from afar, if you are really captivated and would like to see them up close, please read the information described in the next daytrip. In another 0.5 mile (13) the town of Dunquin offers a pottery shop, a café, and B&Bs. Just beyond town 0.5 mile (13.5) is an IYH hostel. The road turns away from Blasket Sound after 1 mile (14.5), and you get a last good look at the Blasket Islands. In 2 miles (16.5) you'll reach a **pottery studio**. Though all pottery is dependent on one's taste, this shop does turn out some fine handthrown pottery. Even better, the studio will ship to any country.

After 2 more miles (18.5) **Ballyferriter** offers a post office, cafés, a pub, a craft shop, and a folk museum. All of these are easy to find since there is essentially only one street through town. In 1.5 miles from town (20), just past the iron-rail bridge, turn **right** up the narrow lane and go 0.25 mile to **Reask**. Only excavated in the last several years, Reask gives a fairly good impression of the layout of a typical monastery from the seventh and eighth centuries. The large stone cross near the entrance is delicately inscribed and is definitely worth a look.

Back at the main road go **right** 0.5 mile (20.5), then go **left** at the sign for **Gallarus Castle and Oratory**. A mile down this junction (21.5) is a **left-right fork**. Turn **right** and go straight up the hill to Gallarus Oratory. Gallarus is a well-preserved piece of architecture that dates to the eighth century. There is a low door in the shape of an inverted V through which you can enter. The mortarless construction, its most important structural feature, has stood, without leaking, for over a thousand years.

From Gallarus, continue up the **extremely steep** 0.5-mile (23.5) hill to the main road (**R559**). After turning **left** on this road and going up the hill a bit farther, turn **left again** on the road to **Kilmalkedar Church**. Almost exactly 1 mile (25) from the turn is **Caherdorgan Stone Fort**. There is **no sign** marking the site so look on the left for an opening in the fuchsia hedge and the stone entrance. This is a small fort with a single outer wall, but there are several beehive huts within the enclosure. In another 0.5 mile (25.5) is Kilmalkedar. Though roofless now, this twelfth-century church retains the stone arches that provide entrance into the two-room structure. Surrounding the church is a graveyard through which the walkway to the church runs. A statue of the Virgin Mary next to a large stone cross marks an impressive beginning to the path. On the same lane, just a stone's throw up from here is **St. Brendan's House**, believed to have been home to the clergy of the church in the fifteenth century. To return to Dingle go back up to the main road (**R559**), then turn left for Dingle at the signpost. From here there is an easy 3-mile ride (28.5) to the next left turn, which takes you the final mile back across the bridge and into Dingle (29.5).

DAYTRIP TO THE BLASKET ISLANDS

You could make a boat trip out to the Blaskets a part of the trek around Slea Head outlined in the previous section. However, because there are so many things to stop and see on that trip it would be pretty difficult to get it all in. That is why I suggest a trip to the Blaskets as a separate outing. There are a couple of ways of getting back to the pier from which the boats leave.

One way is to cycle out, following the route described in the first several paragraphs of "Daytrip to Slea Head." If you do so, the round trip distance is about 25 miles. If you've already cycled Slea Head and don't wish to duplicate that trip, it is relatively inexpensive to hire a cab to take you out to the ferry and then pick you up again for the return.

Ferries cross to the islands from Dunquin Pier daily every half hour beginning at 10:00 A.M., weather permitting. The trip can take anywhere from forty-five minutes to over an hour, depending on sea conditions. The boats are rather small, holding about thirty to forty people and they toss quite a bit when the sea is less than calm. However, the crew is friendly and experienced and the boats are well-equipped with safety equipment.

The Great Blasket is the island on which you will be dropped, and it is part of the chain which is the most westerly land in Europe. On the island there are very few services; the last full-time inhabitants left in 1953. I suppose that is what makes for most of the island's charm. There is no electricity, no cars, no asphalt, and only a few standing buildings.

A **hand-painted map** points out the location of some of the still standing (barely) structures. Although now roofless, the houses of **Tomas O'Crohan** and **Peig Sayers** can be found, as well as a building used as a **school**. Trails lead off in several directions and you can follow them to get even better glimpses out into the farthest reaches of the Atlantic. The beach, **White Strand**, is extraordinarily clean and you can walk down to it and stroll along its length. Some sheep, a few wild donkeys, the sea birds, and possibly some seals on the beach are the extent of what is on the island. It's a great place.

As of this writing there was one **craft shop**, which featured handmade woolens, and one **café**, specializing in homemade lunches. On chilly days (most of them), there will be a peat fire glowing on the hearth. Indeed, it is highly likely that if you take a morning ferry to the island, you will be riding with the café's cook as she brings supplies over from the mainland.

■■■■■■■■■■■■■■■■■■■■■■■■■■■■■■■■■■

TOUR 11
DINGLE TO TRALEE

Distance: 29.5 miles
Estimated time: 1 day
Terrain: Extreme climb at beginning, then becomes relatively flat

After a difficult climb up Conor Pass at the start of this ride, the hills become easier as you work toward Tralee. Along the way you'll have frequent views of Tralee Bay to the north and west.

CONNECTIONS. By bike, Dingle is reached by completing Tour 10. Dingle is also accessible by bus from Tralee, Limerick, Cork, and Killarney.

DINGLE TO TRALEE (29.5 MILES)

Leave Dingle heading northeast on the road out of town to **Conor Pass**. The road is called **R559 (T68)**, but the sign just indicates Conor Pass. The pass is the shortest and most scenic route to take to Tralee as it scales the mountains outside of Dingle. This is a truly **steep** climb. Granted, maybe you've never raced with a peloton through the Pyrenees or sprinted with the pros down the *Champs Élysées*, but, with a bike loaded with clothes and equipment, Conor Pass is really a test.

The occasional herd of cattle being moved from one field to another gives cyclists a chance for an unexpected break.

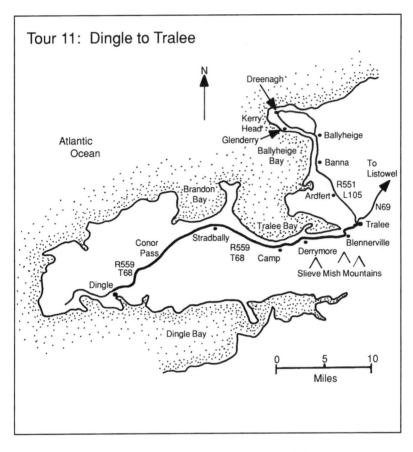

Tour 11: Dingle to Tralee

On the best of days, it is sunny, windy, and only mildly chilly. On cloudier days it may be frigid with gusty winds, especially at the summit 4.5 miles up. There are ways around the pass, but the views of Dingle Bay back to the south and Brandon and Tralee bays to the northeast make this a special climb. Stop at the pullover at the top to take in the view and give yourself a much needed rest. This is also a good place to note the admiring, envious look of motorists who pass by. You can almost see them saying, "Wow, what an athlete that cyclist is!" (Chances are they're actually substituting the words "crazy fool" for "athlete.") As if this weren't reward enough, then there is the **narrow, curvy descent** of 3.5 miles to the base of the mountains. About **halfway down** there is a nice **waterfall** off to the right that is worth a look, if you can squeeze your brakes hard enough to stop. At the bottom (8.5) of the mountain the road sign points to Tralee. Continue in that direction. After 5 miles of comparatively easy terrain you come to **Stradbally** (13.5), where you find the first pub since Dingle and a hostel. Stradbally Strand is nearby, a nice quiet stretch of sand with shallow water and gentle waves, a good place to cool tired feet.

In 2.5 miles (16), near a petrol station and shop, a **campground** sits on the left. From here, the road to Tralee follows right along the edge of Tralee Bay and passes through the crossroads village of **Camp** and the small town of **Derrymore**. Along the route are scattered pubs and B&Bs, but there is very little in the way of services until you get to **Blennerville**, which is 14.5 miles (28) beyond Stradbally.

Just through Blennerville, go **right** over the first bridge onto **N86**. Continue on to the Tralee town center another 1.5 miles (29.5) from the bridge.

TRALEE

" . . . a town whose main redeeming feature is its bus to Dingle. . . . " This is what one prominent guide to Europe has to say about Tralee, population 18,000. Another mentioned Tralee only once, in a sentence describing the road from Dingle to Limerick. Whoever penned those lines certainly did not spend enough time in the rather vibrant, cultured Tralee that is home to some of the best entertainment in all of Ireland. I believe that many times full credit is not given to Tralee's fine array of sites and activities. Not only is this the home of the National Folk Theatre of Ireland; in summer it also hosts the Rose of Tralee Festival, the largest festival in the country, complete with music, food, and the crowning of the Rose of Tralee. These offerings, as well as its impressive shopping district, racetrack, and proximity to the coast, make it well worth a stay of at least a day or two. And that's not even counting Tralee's wealth of relatively untouristed pubs.

As the other books note, Tralee is indeed a major stopover for buses and an important link among several cities; because of its location, traffic passes through here bound to and from Dingle, Killarney, and Limerick. If you intend to leave the circuit of tours described in this book, Tralee is definitely a good place by which to exit. Bus and rail service are both convenient and rather frequent.

As you enter town on the road from Blennerville (**N86**, otherwise called **Canal Road**), go **left** on Prince's Quay. Go past the **town hall** on the right and past a large carpark. Immediately after the carpark turn right on **Ivy Terrace**. **The National Folk Theatre** (*Siamsa Tíre*, described later) is up ahead on the right and the "*i*" is in **Ashe Memorial Hall** just a bit farther up on the right. The "*i*" offers a well-marked map of the city along with souvenirs, informational pamphlets, and the standard books and maps found in any Irish tourist office. It's fairly important to pick up the city map since Tralee is not laid out on a nice north–south, east–west grid.

The main north–south road in the downtown region is **Denny Street**, which leads north away from Ashe Hall. In about two blocks, Denny intersects with **The Mall**, which runs west, and **Castle Street**, which runs east. At this junction, Denny veers to the northeast and becomes **Ashe Street**.

Cyclists struggle to finish the last steep section of the arduous climb up Conor Pass.

The **bus station** (phone 23566; Tralee's prefix is 066) is a block east of Ashe Street's northerly limit. This is also where the **Irish Rail** platform is located (phone 23522). There are a number of **bike shops** in Tralee as well as places to rent bikes. The **post office** is found on Edward Street about a block north of Castle Street. There are plenty of accommodations, including B&Bs and an IHH hostel.

Of all the reasons to come to Tralee, the **National Folk Theatre of Ireland**, *Siamsa Tire* (pronounced *shee-am-sah-tee-reh*), is far and away the best one. If you are anywhere in the vicinity and haven't decided whether to come to Tralee or not, let this be your deciding factor. And if you happen to end up in Tralee on a day the theater is not open, take in the daytrip outlined later in order to justify staying an extra day. But by all means go to this show if you have any interest in Irish folklife whatsoever. For a very reasonable price, a dance/theater company presents a show depicting diverse aspects of Irish folklife from days past. The entire show, sung in Gaelic, revolves around such simple activities as churning butter and thatching the roof of a house. The show also delves into some of the folktales and customs that were part of rural Irish life for many centuries.

Note: The show is meant to be understood by persons of any nationality. Because the show is completely mimed and sung, it's pretty easy to figure out what's going on, even if you can't understand the words.

Though this is the national theater, the building only seats a few hundred people, so call in advance if at all possible to reserve tickets (phone 23055). During the summer months, tour operators purchase large blocks of tickets and shows sell out frequently. Even if you're told on the phone that the show is booked, try going to the box office in person. Many times, afternoon cancellations make a few tickets available. During July and August there are shows every day except Sunday but the schedule is a little more restrictive at other times of the year. Please call to confirm show dates.

In the **Town Park** in which the *"i"* is located is a beautiful garden with several varieties of roses, enough to remind you that this is the home of the **Rose of Tralee Festival**. The **greyhound track** is found on **Brewery Road**. To get there take **Edward Street** north past the rail and bus station. In under a half mile turn left on Brewery Road. The track is another half mile away on the right. Racing is held Tuesday and Friday evenings beginning at 8:00 P.M.

DAYTRIP TO KERRY HEAD (34.5 MILES ROUND TRIP)

Kerry Head is a resistant chunk of land jutting into the Atlantic some 17 miles northwest of Tralee. Looking like a lifted pinky finger on a cup of tea, the Kerry Head peninsula forms the northern coast of **Ballyheige Bay** and the southern flank of the **Shannon River** as it empties into the ocean. While rather long compared to most daytrips in this book, the 34.5-mile loop certainly merits your time and energy. While some may choose to ignore this trip in favor of heading north to grander attractions, if you stay in Tralee an extra day in order to catch the greyhound races or the folk theater, there is no better way to spend your time than cycling out to Kerry Head.

To get there take **R551 (L105)** to the northwest following signs to Ardfert or Ballyheige. The road is not particularly impressive until you get to the historically significant town of Ardfert 5.5 miles away. Ardfert originally served as a mission site in the sixth century, and St. Brendan eventually founded a monastery here as well. The Fitzmaurice family, an important Kerry lineage from the 1200s to the 1600s, held power and also founded a friary in Ardfert.

The most striking feature remaining in town is **Ardfert Cathedral**, built in the mid-thirteenth century. It has a number of interesting architectural features. Most apparent are the rows of long, slender windows that line the walls. The cathedral is also rather large compared to many that are still standing. A fairly well-preserved double-stone arch acts as the entrance to the chancel area. Some very fine stone carvings are found occasionally along the walls of the chapel. At the time of this writing major renovations were still ongoing on the cathedral grounds.

Continuing northwest on **R551** out of Ardfert, in 1.5 miles (7) you'll come to a turnoff to the left to **Banna Strand**. The beach is not far from this point, and the views of both Tralee Bay and Ballyheige Bay are superb. Nearby you can see a monument commemorating Sir Roger Casement's landing on the Good Friday before the 1916 Easter Rising. Casement was attempting to bring a load of German guns in for the rebellion but, with communications gone sour, the plot failed and he was arrested near this spot by the British.

Back on **R551** proceed the remaining 5 miles (12) to the tiny village of Ballyheige, which is nicely situated on the shore of Ballyheige Bay. There is a lovely beach here and terrific views across Tralee Bay to the Dingle peninsula and the **Magharee Islands**, otherwise called the Seven Hogs. From here the road extends to the west and in 3 more miles (15) reaches another hamlet, Glenderry. Beyond Glenderry the cliffs become more rugged and rocky. The black-and-white Holstein cattle pasturing on the shallow, verdant slopes are effectively fenced by the sea; their lush dinner plate extends nearly to the edge.

Two miles farther (17) is the village of Dreenagh, which is the westernmost point of Kerry Head. From here the view shifts to the north toward the mouth of the River Shannon and Loop Head on County Clare's coast as the road follows the northern, bouldered edge of the peninsula. In 3.5 miles (20.5) the path pulls back inland, and in another 2 miles (22.5) you return to Ballyheige. The rest of the 12 miles involve retracing your route back to Tralee.

Friendly ferry operators easily accommodate bikes on their frequent trips to the three Aran Islands. Photo by Jeff Kirchhoff

■ ■

TOUR 12

TRALEE TO LAHINCH

Distance: 61 miles
Estimated time: 1–2 days
Terrain: Flat to moderately rolling

The flat farmlands of the early part of this ride are broken up by a ferry crossing of the River Shannon. After ferrying across, you follow the road back to the coast and the popular resort town of Lahinch.

CONNECTIONS. To reach Tralee by bike, follow the route described in Tour 11. Because Tralee is somewhat of a transportation hub, it is readily accessible by both bus and train from many different locations.

TRALEE TO KILRUSH (34.5 MILES)

Leave Tralee **north** on **N69 (T68)**. The road skirts the base of **Stack's Mountains**, which rise off to the east for about half of the 16 miles to the town of Listowel. Most of the distance is on a **fairly busy road** through moderately rolling hills, although the first 4.5 miles out of town is a long slow climb. Farmland dominates the landscape to the west of the mountains making for pleasant, though not dramatic, scenery.

Listowel is large enough to offer a variety of services including a **bike shop**, foodstores, B&Bs, banks, and pubs. On the main square in the center of town is **St. John's Art and Heritage Centre**. Located in what used to be a Church of Ireland building, the art center now houses a tourist office (phone 068 22590), a small theater that is now the site of musical performances, art exhibits, and a creative-writing workshop. At the information desk you can obtain for a very small charge a booklet that describes a walking tour of the town.

In moving on toward Tarbert, follow the signs carefully through town. Because of the one-way streets, you wind your way in almost a full circle before climbing the last hill out of town. There is somewhat **less traffic** on the ride from Listowel, and the hills are less severe than those leading to it. Much of the traffic that came into Listowel veered off at the crossroads in town and headed to Limerick. This inland route is again rather dull when contrasted to the western coastline, but it is the most direct route to Tarbert and the ferry crossing the River Shannon. Eleven miles from Listowel (27) bring you to the town of Tarbert. Follow the signs through the village to the ferry, which is another 2 miles (29) beyond town. Ferries leave **every hour on the half hour** from 7:00 A.M. to 9:00 P.M., and the system is very efficiently and courteously run. Crossings take about twenty minutes and provide an excellent shortcut across the river. The alternative is to ride to Limerick and go around the river.

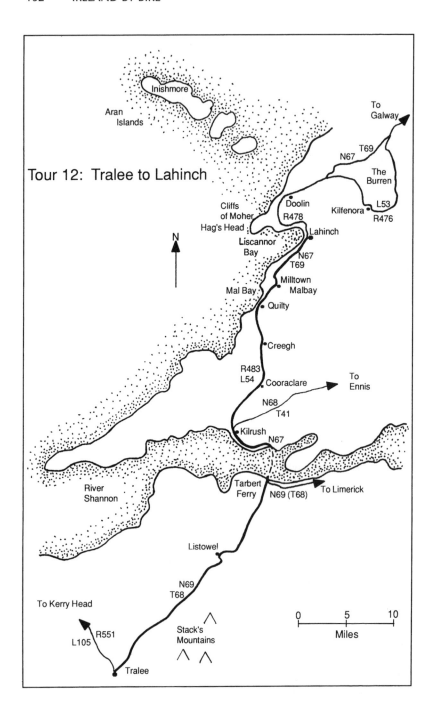

Tour 12: Tralee to Lahinch

Tarbert Ferry is an easy, inexpensive way to cross the River Shannon and save valuable time.

After crossing the river you are in County Clare. Follow the **N67** west toward Kilrush. After you leave the ferry the road follows the River Shannon for some time and passes by a large power project. From the ferry it is another 5.5 miles (34.5) to Kilrush.

KILRUSH

Although at first glance Kilrush is a quiet little town, when you turn left into the main square you find that this is actually a busy market town. Though it bears little resemblance to its name in the Irish, *Cil Rois*, or "Church of the Wood," when originally founded Kilrush was nestled among the forests and woods of the Shannon Valley.

After taking a **left** into Kilrush from **N67** you come into the downtown plaza with the town hall standing in the center. Surrounding this are a number of businesses including banks, B&Bs, restaurants, pubs, newsagents, and foodstores. There is also a **tourist information office, a bike shop,** and an independent hostel located in town.

KILRUSH TO LAHINCH (26.5 MILES)

To leave Kilrush go around to the **north** side of the square and take the road marked to Ennis. In a short distance take **R483 (L54)** which is signposted to Cooraclare. The road to Cooraclare is fairly hilly coming out of Kilrush but moderates in a couple of miles. Cooraclare, 5 miles (39.5) from Kilrush, has a couple of B&Bs, a pub, a foodstore and that's about it. Four miles beyond (43.5) is Creegh, which is about the same size and offers about the same number of services. The road continues for 6 more miles (49.5) of rather easy pedaling to Quilty. Most of the distance from Kilrush to Quilty follows land that is used for cow and sheep pasture and for cutting hay. But once in Quilty you are back at the coast.

> *Ah! seaweed smells from sandy caves*
> *And thyme and mist in whiffs,*
> *In-coming tide, Atlantic waves*
> *Slapping the sunny cliffs, Lark song and sea sounds in the air*
> *And splendour, splendour everywhere.*

Thus wrote Sir John Betjeman. I don't know if he was standing at Quilty looking out or not, but he easily could have been.

Hanging out at the Cliffs of Moher. It's amazing how "up close and personal" you can get to some of Ireland's unique treasures. Photo by Jeff Kirchhoff

It's amazing how quickly both the scenery and the weather change when you move from inland to shoreline. The wind picks up and instead of being intermingled with "eau de cow," the smells of fish and salt and wet sand pervade the air. Instead of the sharp, striking division of blue sky and green grass, the view out over the Atlantic from here is a canvas of a dozen shades of blues and grays finely meshed together on the horizon (assuming it's not raining).

Continue to the **right** on **R483**, which essentially follows the Clare coastline for the remaining 4 miles (53.5) to the small resort town of Milltown Malbay. Before arriving in Milltown you can take the marked detour to **Spanish Point**, which is a tiny spit of land thrust out into **Mal Bay**. It connects back to the Lahinch road just northwest of Milltown. The point gets its name from an occasion in 1588 when some shipwreck survivors of the Spanish Armada were executed by a local sheriff. Here is a nice view of the Atlantic and **Silver Strand**, a popular spot for swimming. The road to Spanish Point is marked as the **Coastal Road** and will bypass the downtown area of Milltown.

Milltown itself has some very nice B&Bs that have views of the ocean, and the residents can also recommend a fine pub or two. Most recently Milltown has made itself famous as a heritage center for the traditional music and dance of West Clare.

Just through town take **N67** (**T69**) left to Lahinch. The road traces the shore of **Liscannor Bay** for the next several miles, and as you cycle farther north you begin to see **Hag's Head**, home of the Cliffs of Moher, in the distance. Lahinch is 7.5 miles (61) from Milltown Malbay and is a perfect place to stop and relax for a day or two.

LAHINCH

The original name of Lahinch, *Leath Inse*, means "peninsula," but in Irish the town is called *Leacht Ui Chonchuir*, which means "O'Connor's Grave." Lahinch has earned its fame today as a spirited seaside resort town. A concrete promenade situated between the strand and the town acts as a meeting place for members of various generations and also serves to give the town an almost Atlantic City-like feel (albeit much, much smaller). The beach is long and relatively free of debris, the water is cold, and the waves are sometimes big enough to surf. The lifeguard stands on the beach are testament that it does at times get sunny enough to swim.

Besides the typical offerings, B&Bs, a hostel, and restaurants, there is an entertainment center near the beach that is open during most of the summer and offers a number of different activities. There are also two extremely beautiful golf courses that are both open to the public.

■■■■■■■■■■■■■■■■■■■■■■■■■■■■■■■■■■

TOUR 13
LAHINCH TO DOOLIN

Distance: 12 miles
Estimated time: 1 day
Terrain: A lot of climbing at the beginning, more downhill during the latter half

Though a short tour by bike, this trip is loaded with interesting, scenic, and historic attractions. Along the way you can see the famous Cliffs of Moher, visit a town popular for its traditional music, and, time permitting, take a boat to the Aran Islands.

If you follow the tours in order from here, after Doolin you will end up in Galway. However, it is possible to treat the ride from Lahinch to Doolin as a daytrip rather than as a separate tour. In that case you will return to Lahinch. If you choose this option, please follow the "Alternate Route to the Burren" listed at the end of this chapter. Then you will pick up Tour 14 in progress and continue on to Galway.

CONNECTIONS. Lahinch is reached by bike via Tour 12. Because it is relatively close to Shannon Airport (a bit over 30 miles), it is also a prime location from which to start your tour of Ireland. Buses from Limerick are available to Lahinch as well.

LAHINCH TO DOOLIN (12 MILES)
The road to Doolin from Lahinch is **R478 (L54)**, which leaves Lahinch by following the outer boundary of the golf course. Just beyond the beach at the north end of the course the road winds back to the west and stays along the shore of **Liscannor Bay** for just over 1 mile. Past the village of Liscannor, 3.5 miles from Lahinch, is a **camping park** off to the left. In another 1.5 miles (5), on the rather steep ascent of the hills leading to the Cliffs of Moher, is an **independent hostel**. Another 1.5 miles (6.5) bring you to the **left turn** into the visitors center of the **Cliffs of Moher**. There's an information office as well as toilets, a restaurant, and plenty of souvenirs.

The Cliffs, often photographed and heavily visited by tourists, are truly some of the most magnificent walls of rock to be found anywhere on the island. Rising to a height of almost 600 feet above the Atlantic, the cliffs bear the full brunt of the ocean's waved fury. A number of species of birds nest on their sheer walls, and with binoculars or a zoom lens on a camera you can see them fairly well. The name "Moher" comes from an ancient fort that once occupied the site but which was destroyed during the time of Napoleon.

From the carpark a path leads up to **O'Brien's Tower,** where, for a small

Whistling (and fiddling around) while you work at the Cliffs of Moher; itinerant musicians are a common part of the Irish landscape.

admission charge, you can climb up for a better view of the panorama below. There's a telescope on top of the tower to help you get a look at the seabirds on the cliffs and at the Aran Islands to the north. From the tower it's also possible to look back on Liscannor Bay and Lahinch. If you follow one of the paths leading south away from the tower you can look back on the cliff where the tower sits. This cliff happens to be the highest of all of them. Out in the Atlantic just west of the tower is a **rock pillar** about 200 feet tall called Breanan Mor.

Back on the road about 0.5 mile (7) up from the carpark at the crest of the hill is a splendid view of the Aran Islands and Galway Bay far to the north. On the left 3 miles farther (10) is a sign pointing toward **camping** in Doolin. The main entrance into Doolin, however, is another 2 miles (12) down the road.

DOOLIN

You may find it unusual that a tiny town like this, which is even confused about its own name (it's often called Fisherstreet), rates an entire tour. However, if you get the opportunity to spend some time here you'll see why. Though its traditional economic backbone is, like so many other parts of the country, based on fishing, Doolin has made quite a name for itself in pubs, Irish folk music, and as a jumping-off point to the Aran Islands. If you have enough time, Doolin is also a good base from which to explore the Burren area to the northeast.

There are two ways to get into Doolin from the "cliffs" road. The first is the road described above that leads to camping. The second entrance is a **left** at the petrol station/foodstore about a mile beyond the first turnoff. Down this road a little over 1 mile take a **left**, and you are on the one and only street in Doolin.

The most famous of Doolin's pubs is **Gus O'Connor's**. It's found just down the road after making the left into town. Nearly every night the place is packed with people, some of whom have traveled for days to come specifically to this spot. The music really is *that* good, that is, if you enjoy the tin whistle, *bodhran*, and other traditional instruments played quite masterfully. The only drawbacks to the pub's popularity are that you probably won't find a place to sit and there's a good chance you'll only have about one square foot of space to stand in. Half the crowd seems to hold its drinks raised in a toast, but in fact the only room to hold your drink is up high.

For a potentially quieter, less boisterous pint of stout try **McDermott's** or **McMann's**, which are both to the east of town a short distance. Near these two pubs there are also a couple of reasonably priced restaurants.

Historic sites of interest in and around Doolin include **Dunmacfelim Castle**, an O'Connor castle built in the early 1500s and later taken over by the O'Brien clan. **Doolin House**, which is now in ruins because of a fire, was built in 1778. Its main claim to historical fame is that several authors, including J. M. Synge and George Bernard Shaw, visited friends here regularly. The fifteenth-century **Killilagh Church** has an impressive chiseled arch, but some of its more interesting architecture has been removed and displayed in other locations. Finally, there is **Toomullen Church**. Though not much is left at the site, the remains of this church are over fifteen hundred years old. All of these structures lie within minutes of each other and all are close to the businesses in downtown Doolin.

DAYTRIP TO INISHEER (ARAN ISLANDS, COUNTY GALWAY)

The Arans will be the final stronghold of the Celts. Many leave but many come back after taking their fling at the world beyond and all its confusion, shoving, and poverty . . . Those who go never get the sound of the sea from their ears or the sight of it from their dreams. They return to these forlorn rocks, for only here is there true peace.

Leon Uris, in his book *Ireland: A Terrible Beauty*, wrote these words about the three Aran Islands located off the west coast of Ireland. The islands truly are a refuge from the sounds and sights of modernity. On Inisheer, smallest and easternmost of the islands, though time has not exactly stood still, there is still ample evidence of the past. There are a number of interesting buildings, and the ancient utility boat, the *curragh*, is still seen in use around the island. A *curragh*, little more than a wooden frame covered in canvas and pitch, resembles a large canoe. Because it's so light, it bounces in a hair-raising fashion from wave to wave and is paddled with two oars that are essentially long boards with little or no blade.

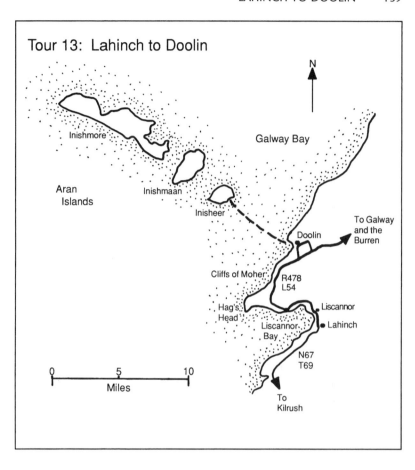

Tour 13: Lahinch to Doolin

N

Galway Bay

Inishmore

Aran
Islands

Inishmaan

Inisheer

To Galway
and the
Burren

Doolin

Cliffs of Moher

R478
L54

Hag's
Head

Liscannor

Lahinch

Liscannor
Bay

N67
T69

0   5   10

Miles

To
Kilrush

Not far from Inisheer's pier, which is on the north side of the island, is *Cnoc Raithni*, an ancient mound dating back to 2000 B.C. To the southeast is *Dun Formna*, the remains of an O'Brien family castle built in the fourteenth century. This is a good landmark; it sits on a hill and rises well above most of the surrounding countryside. A climb to the top gives you a nice view of the patchwork fields and the stone fences that serve to divide them. Inisheer's beach, *An Tra*, is a beautiful white color, clean and safe for swimming if you can stand the cold. Perhaps the best way to see all the island has to offer is to follow the walking path, **The *Inis Oirr* Way**, which runs essentially east and west across the island and loops its way past all of the island's best sights.

To get to Inisheer from Doolin take one of the **Doolin Ferries** from Doolin Pier not far from the center of town. The crossing to Inisheer is less than 5 miles and is generally completed in a half hour. In June, July, and August boats leave several times a day beginning at around 9:30 A.M. with the last boat going out

Road signs often leave little to the imagination.

at 7:30 P.M. The ferry will transport your bike, but unless you plan to spend the night on the island (there are accommodations available), there's not much need to take it. Considering that the island is only fourteen hundred acres in size, it's small enough to explore easily by foot. Boats also go out to Inishmore, the largest island, but I recommend waiting until you get to Galway before making that trip.

ALTERNATE ROUTE TO THE BURREN

If you have chosen to cycle to the Cliffs of Moher and/or to Doolin as a daytrip out of Lahinch you can use this **alternate route** to connect up with Tour 14 without having to retrace any of your "steps." Having cycled up to the Cliffs you already know that doing it again would not exactly be fun. It's quite a lot of climbing. Anyway, this tour gives directions to the **Burren Display Centre** which is in Kilfenora. At the end of this section please skip to that portion of Tour 14, which is marked with the heading, "Burren Tour."

At the **east** edge of Lahinch **follow the signs** to Ennistymon. The road has some pretty serious **climbing** for part of the 2.5 miles to town. Ennistymon has all services available. Across the **bridge** and into the town center go **left** (opposite of the road to Ennis). Follow the road up the **steep hill** for about 0.5 mile (3). Just after the hill crests and you begin to descend, take the **right fork** posted to Kilfenora.

The road winds and climbs for another 0.5 mile (3.5) until finally leveling off. The next 2 miles into Kilfenora (5.5) are an easy ride. Follow the road into town until you get to the Burren Display Centre which is found on your left.

■ ■

TOUR 14
DOOLIN TO GALWAY

Distance: 49.5 miles
Estimated time: 1–2 days
Terrain: Very hilly during the first half of the trip, becoming moderately hilly to flat

Some of the most unusual terrain in Ireland lies just to the northeast of Doolin and is a part of this tour. Known as the Burren, the area has a rocky, seemingly desolate appearance. After passing through the Burren, the route brings you to the coast of Galway Bay and follows the shoreline the rest of the way into Galway.

CONNECTIONS. Doolin can be reached by bike by completing Tour 13. Bus service is available but not frequent to Doolin from Limerick. Boats pass regularly to and from Doolin Pier from the Aran Islands. Galway can be reached by train from Limerick or Dublin and is a good place to begin if you have limited time and want to see the northwest.

DOOLIN TO BALLYVAUGHAN (18.5 MILES)

Leave Doolin via **R478**, which is the road you were on when you turned toward Doolin. Travel east on this road. At the crossroads in 1.5 miles continue **straight** on the road to Lisdoonvarna. After another mile in Lisdoonvarna (2.5) veer to the **right** on **R476 (L53)**, following signs to Kilfenora. This route cuts through the conifers and willows of **Ballykeel** (*An Baile Caol*) **Forest** for 3 miles (5.5). Soon after you pass the forest, a mile-long descent takes you to Kilfenora (6.5). Go **straight** into town, then turn **right** in town for the **Burren Display Centre.**

Burren Tour. The Display Centre is a combination tourist office, gift shop, and interpretive center and it offers an audio-visual program describing the Burren's wildflowers and geologic history. This is also a good spot to pick up informational literature about the Burren.

Kilfenora offers two or three places to buy food and refreshments, and just down the hill past the Display Centre is a small **bike shop**. Just behind the Display Centre is **Kilfenora Cathedral**, which was built in the twelfth century. Although roofless, like most of the ruins of this age, the cathedral has numerous points of architectural interest. There are scalloped forms and carvings, stone effigies of early church leaders, and wall tombs. Directly to the rear of the church is the twelfth century Doorty cross, a very interesting structure with religious carvings on both sides. A bit farther to the west, in a nearby field is a 13-foot high cross with a carving of the crucifixion on its east side.

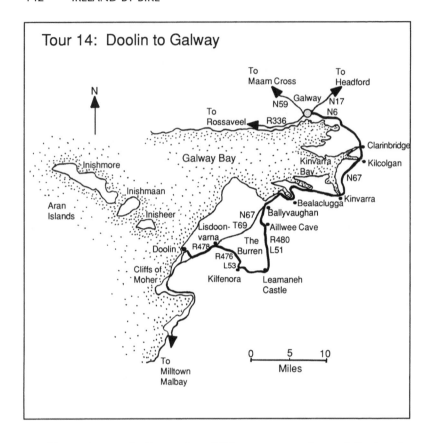

Tour 14: Doolin to Galway

To continue to the Burren from Kilfenora, go out of town **following the road** marked to Ennis (**R476, L53**). Beyond this point 3.5 miles (10), veer **left** on the Ballyvaughan road (**R480, L51**). At the **junction** you will find **Leamaneh Castle**. The tower house on the northeast side of the building dates to about the fifteenth century while the rest of the house was added in the seventeenth century. Notice the slit-like windows of the earlier structure and the more open views of the newer windows. At one time you could explore around the inside rooms, but as of this writing, because the castle sits on private grounds, it is closed to the public.

From a distance, the most obvious sign that you are beginning to enter the Burren are the great slabs of rock that constitute most of the landscape. Because of the redundantly gray, pockmarked texture of these limestone rocks, the Burren gives a first impression of a gloomy, lifeless rockscape. But when you get closer, you find that this sensation is unfounded. Between and around these jutting planks of rock are dozens of species of ferns and wildflowers.

In fact, botanists are quite amazed at the variety of plants growing in this alkaline soil. Indeed, over three-quarters of all of Ireland's plant species are found in the 100-square-mile Burren outback. Most of these are not tall, highly visible flowers. Many require you to walk around and get a closer look. If you do you may find a number of different types of orchids, Mediterranean ferns, arctic wildflowers, and a whole host of others. Though scientists have a number of different theories to explain this unusual diversity, for tourists the benefits are strictly aesthetic.

Nearly 3 miles (13) beyond the castle is **Carran Church**, which is of fifteenth-century origin. The path to the church takes you through a cow pasture (literally) to a stile entering the church graveyard. A beautiful, low stone portal is the main ingress to the church.

Down the road 2 miles (15) see the **Poulnabrone Dolmen** (or Portal Dolmen), an ancient grave built about four thousand years ago. Notice also the mini-dolmens created by tourists and locals and scattered around the Burren terrain. Though technically the road entered into the Burren some miles back, this is really your first opportunity to amble around and get a close look at many of the unique ferns and flowers.

In 1.5 miles (16.5) you come to **Gleninsheen Wedge Tomb**. Located on the southwest slope of **Aillwee Mountain**, the ancient stone tomb dates back to the Bronze Age and is most famous for the centuries-old gold collar that was found here in 1930. Soon after this is a **fast**, 2.5-mile descent (19) to the **turn-off** for **Aillwee Cave**. Though not one of the largest caves in the world, Aillwee is worth touring. There are some interesting formations inside, including a beautiful waterfall, and the cave goes back for several thousand feet. There is an admission charge and tours leave on a regular basis. One of the best features of the cave is its entrance, an award-winning design of limestone rocks that blends in beautifully with the surroundings. As you approach the cave you will find a place to lock your bike, as well as lockers for stowing gear.

Return to the main road, and at the junction in 0.5 mile (17), go **right** toward Ballyvaughan. In 1.5 miles (18.5) is the town center. If you're ready for a break there are pubs, B&Bs, foodstores, and a craft shop or two here.

BALLYVAUGHAN TO GALWAY (31 MILES)

To continue, turn **right** at the Galway signpost on N67 (**T69**). For 4.5 miles (23) the road is sandwiched between the hills of the Burren on the right and Galway Bay to the left. At **Bell Harbor** (*Bealaclugga*) the road forks left and the road sign points to Kinvarra. Here you leave behind the Burren landscape. In 5.5 miles (28.5) you pass the *Cead Mile Failte* sign welcoming you to County Galway and the west of Ireland. In 2.5 miles (31) a sign points left for an **IYH hostel**. After 1.5 more miles (32.5) you enter Kinvarra. This tiny village is perfectly situated at the tip of Kinvarra Bay and the grassy, no-cars-allowed pier is a nice spot for a picnic lunch. In town there are pubs, foodstores, and a pay phone.

If you've had enough riding for the day there are also B&Bs available.

Past town center 1.5 miles (34) is **Dunguaire Castle**, a sixteenth-century castle sitting right on the edge of the bay. The castle has been completely restored and now hosts medieval banquets, Irish music, and dancing. For reservations or more information about the banquets talk to your travel agent or call the Castle Banquet reservation number in the United States at 800-243-8687.

A gently rolling 6 miles (40) take you to the town of Kilcolgan, where you take the **left** fork on **N18** to Galway. In 1.5 miles (41.5) you come to Clarinbridge, the self-proclaimed "Oyster Country" of Ireland, with several taverns where you can sample a plateful of the slippery bivalves.

The road to Galway continues **straight** through Clarinbridge, and in 4 miles (45.5) you come to a roundabout. Follow the signs for Galway (**N6**). A "dual carriageway" (four-lane highway) begins in 2.5 miles (48) with nice wide shoulders and plenty of room for a bike to get out of traffic. The four lanes eventually end, but the good shoulder lasts most of the rest of the 1.5 miles (49.5) into Galway.

GALWAY

The Galway of today is the unofficial capital of the west of Ireland, the entrance to the Connemara region, and the largest city in County Galway with a population of around 57,000. Known in Irish as *Gaillimh* (pronounced *galliv*), Galway is a fun city. It seems to attract all sorts of people, from families together on holiday to European backpackers to, of course, lots of cyclists. Just sit in Eyre (pronounced *air*) Square, the main downtown park, and watch as the scores of people pass by. The sidewalks in the town center swell with people, and there are lots of crosswalks, evidence that pedestrians have some leverage over the cars. Streets such as Shop, Quay, and Market are heavily lined with all sorts of shops, both for tourists and locals. There are a number of **bike shops** and **bike rental facilities** in Galway. You should have no trouble finding repair or replacement parts.

Tiny lanes often connect two streets, and these are often full of unique and interesting shops. The crush of people and buildings leaves little room for the stores on these smaller streets to advertise, so necessity has prompted a solution. Kids are hired to sit and hold signs along the main thoroughfares telling the public of the deals and bargains that can be found only a block or two away.

Galway, perhaps because of its size and its popularity with visitors, seems a bit more cosmopolitan than many other parts of the country. And it is, at least on the surface, a thriving, vital city. Street players materialize at almost every corner, and music pervades the air downtown; on one corner it might be bagpipes, on another a bodhran drum and tin whistle, while down the street, guitar and saxophone players do their best to add to the cacophony of sounds.

The city's name comes from the river running through town, *Abhainn na*

Gaillimh, or Galway River (although on maps it is known as the River Corrib). The river is so named because it was here that Gailleamh, the daughter of a legendary Irish figure, drowned.

The original settlements on this spot included a Norman castle that was built in the thirteenth century. Because of its location on Galway Bay, the city's size and population grew quickly, and toward the end of the fifteenth century Galway was chartered as an independent city. Several families or tribes dominated the government of the city for nearly two hundred years.

From the time of the Great Famine in the 1840s until the last forty years or so, Galway experienced general decline. Today, however, because of a renewed interest in the Gaelic language, an increase in its industrial base, improved connections to Shannon and Dublin airports, and increased tourism, Galway is once again a prosperous city.

Galway is found on the northeastern shore of Galway Bay and is the hub of much of County Galway's activities. The River Corrib runs mostly north–south through the western part of downtown and, in turn, empties into the bay. The main shopping district, as well as a number of the local historic sights, are found east of the river.

Pedestrians make great strides in taking over Galway streets.

A fountain sculpture celebrates the hookers of Galway. ("Hookers," incidentally, are traditional Galway sailboats.)

Galway is accessible by train and by bus from Limerick (Shannon Airport) and Dublin. The rail and bus terminals are found together very near the town center at the southeast corner of Eyre Square. You can also fly into and out of Galway via the Dublin, Shannon, and Cork airports. Galway's airport is located east of town on Monivea Road.

As you come into town from the Burren tour on **N6**, the way to the *"i"* (phone 63081; Galway's prefix is 091) is well marked. Just after passing **Eyre Square** where there are likely to be hundreds of people milling about, turn **left** at the **Bank of Ireland** and **Allied Irish Bank**. Besides numerous books about Galway, city maps, and the County Galway guide, you can also purchase tickets for Aran Island boat trips (discussed later) at the tourist office.

Back at Eyre Square, which surrounds John Fitzgerald Kennedy Park, public toilets and pay phones are available. From the northwest edge of the square, **Williamsgate Street** runs to the west and over its length turns into William Street, Shop Street, High Street, and finally Quay Street. The **General Post Office** is just north of William Street, about half a block up **Eglinton Street**.

A helpful and informative publication available at the tourist office is *A Tourist Trail of Old Galway*. This self-directed tour of the oldest parts of the city follows a marked route that takes approximately two hours to complete. **Eyre Square** is the site of a public address President Kennedy gave to the residents of Galway just five months before he was assassinated. The rusty brown sculpture sitting in the central fountain represents Galway's seafaring past. Erected in 1984 to commemorate Galway's quincentennial, the sailboat design of the sculpture and the dark sails commemorate the design of a traditional type of Galway boat, the Galway Hooker. Nearby is a sculpture of Padraic O'Conaire, a Galway-born writer. At the entrance to the square is the **Browne Doorway**, a stone window and doorway removed from a Galway mansion in 1905. The interesting feature of the door is the coat of arms near the top dating to the year 1627.

Travel southwest from Eyre Square on **William Street**, then turn **north** on **Upper Abbeygate** until you reach **Market Street**. Halfway down this block is the **Lynch Memorial Window**. At the top of a stone doorway is a plaque describing the stern justice of Major James Lynch FitzStephen. In 1493, it is said, he convicted and hanged his own son for murdering a Spanish visitor. The legend is somewhat dubious, but it makes for an interesting landmark.

A bit farther down Market, turn **right** on **Bowling Green**. A short way down the street is the house where **Nora Barnacle** lived. Nora's claim to fame is having run off with and married author James Joyce in the early 1900s. Back on Market and a little farther southwest you come to the source of the street's name. On Saturdays, vendors with carts and stalls sell everything from garden vegetables and used books to grilled bratwurst.

Also in this area is the **Collegiate Church of St. Nicholas**, an imposing and somber structure. Built in 1320, the church boasts a number of architecturally

"Little League" hurlers practice at a local field.

and historically engaging features. The heavy stone baptismal font that you see as you enter from the south entrance dates back to the sixteenth or seventeenth century. Still used today, the four-sided font displays a different design on each of its sides. A cobbler's tombstone is imbedded on the west wall, which bears a large Celtic cross. The carved stone dates to 1577. The Crusader's Tomb is a grave slab on the floor of the Chapel of Christ and marks the final resting place of a thirteenth-century crusader. The church gets its name from St. Nicholas of Myra who is the patron of all travelers. Not coincidentally, this is the spot where Christopher Columbus is said to have heard mass before "sailing the ocean blue in 1492." Outside, the rain gutters are designed in the form of gargoyles, featuring a variety of different types of animals.

Spanish Arch, or **Blind Arch**, is the double-arched remains of a city wall built in 1584 and found next door to the **Galway City Museum**, cramped but interesting. The museum houses a number of relics of and pictures showing life in Old Galway. Via an iron staircase you can go up on the roof terrace to get a nice view of the river. The museum is well worth a visit.

Just across **Wolfe Tone Bridge** on the west side of the river was the site of the **Claddagh**, a separate fishing village which for all intents and purposes no longer exists. The people of the Claddagh, living outside the walls of Galway city, were Irish speaking, quite independent, and married mostly within the area. The famous **Claddagh Ring**, named for this village, was originally designed by a man named Joyce who learned goldsmithing while a captive of Algerian pirates. In the early 1700s he returned to the Claddagh and set up shop. Today the ring, with its two hands holding a heart topped by a crown, is a symbol of friendship and love. Traditionally it was used as a wedding ring. Though Claddagh rings can be purchased all over the world, it is considerably more romantic to buy one in the bosom of their origin.

Beautifully situated near the River Corrib, across the **Salmon Weir Bridge,** to the northwest of the city is **Galway Cathedral.** It's fairly easy to find; just look for the distinctive dome on the skyline. Completed in 1965, the cathedral is modern and absolutely lavish. There are tons of stained glass and sculpture. My personal favorites are the intricately detailed tile mosaics. Behind the high altar there is a big mosaic of Christ on the cross with Mary on one side and John on the other. One of the side chapels also features a smaller mosaic of John F. Kennedy.

Besides the ever-present pubs offering a variety of contemporary and traditional music, there are **three theaters** in Galway, each offering its own unique program. **Druid Theater,** found just off Flood Street not far from the museum, offers an assortment of comedy and drama for a reasonable price. Another theater that specializes in plays is the **Punchbag,** located not far from the Druid. The theater offering more traditional and regional productions is *An Taibhdearc* (pronounced *tive yark*). The *Taibhdearc* Company proffers song and dance similar to that of the National Folk Theatre in Tralee as well as programs for special events and festivals. *An Taibhdearc* is located on **Middle Street,** a block northeast of the Druid.

Galway's **greyhound track,** found on **College Road** on the northeast end of town, generally opens for racing on Tuesday and Friday evenings.

DAYTRIP TO ARAN ISLANDS

The two most visited Aran Islands are Inisheer, which is farthest east, and Inishmore, which is largest and farthest west. Both can be reached by boat from Galway. There are several ferry operators housed in the tourist office. Ask around for best prices, fastest service, and most convenient times. The firms offer a number of options, including reasonably priced packages that can include a night on the island in either a hostel or B&B. If you wish to make just a day of it, you can leave for the island in the morning and return later that same day on another boat.

Boats to Inishmore take approximately ninety minutes from the dock in Galway. To get to the docks from the tourist office, walk past the office to the **south** and then turn **right** on **Queen Street.** In two blocks go **left** on **Dock Road,** which will take you directly to the pier where the boats load passengers. *Important note:* A trip to Inisheer is described in the preceding tour under "Daytrip to Inisheer (Aran Islands, County Galway)." A boat trip to Inishmore is described in the following tour, "Galway to Inishmore," with a departure from Rossaveel. If you plan to follow the tours as written in this book, then skip the trip to the islands at this time. However, if you have extra time and would like to spend an additional day in Galway, a trek to Inishmore definitely constitutes a worthwhile diversion.

■

TOUR 15
GALWAY TO INISHMORE

Distance: 23 miles to Rossaveel, then the boat trip to Inishmore
Estimated time: 1 day
Terrain: Flat for much of the way, although some hills the first few miles

In terms of terrain this is the easiest stretch of cycling in this entire book. The road from Galway follows the north shore of Galway Bay the entire distance to the tiny village of Rossaveel. This tour is written with the idea in mind that you have not yet visited Inishmore (the westernmost of the Aran Islands) and that you plan to go there.

CONNECTIONS. Galway is accessible by bike via Tour 14. Flights from Dublin and Shannon airports arrive daily at Galway Airport, located east of the city. Buses and trains service Galway from Dublin as well.

In making the most of your cycling time and your ability to see Ireland's attractions, it is best to travel to Inishmore from Rossaveel rather than from Galway. Not only is the boat trip shorter from there, but the connecting tour to

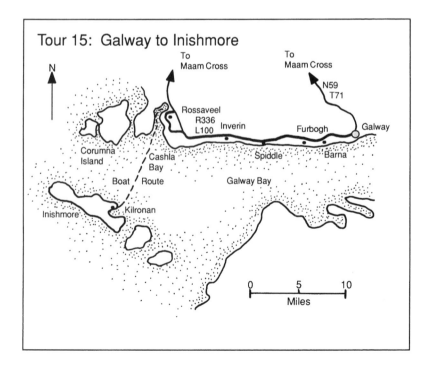

Clifden is much shorter if you break it up in this fashion. So this tour describes the route from Galway to the harbor at Rossaveel and then to the island of Inishmore. Then the following tour picks up again at Rossaveel and takes you farther west–northwest to Clifden.

Please note that it is best to purchase your ticket from Rossaveel to Inishmore while you are in Galway. There is a ticket office in Rossaveel, but it's best to know ahead of time that you have a reserved seat. There are overnight packages available for the Rossaveel-to-Inishmore trip just as there are for the Galway-to-Inishmore trip (see the previous tour for more information).

Boats leave Rossaveel regularly with morning, early afternoon, and evening departures. Check with the ferry companies for specific times. The ride from Galway to Rossaveel is a rather flat 23 miles. If you leave Galway early enough to catch the morning or early afternoon boat, you will have several hours left to tour the island before nightfall. Then you'll be able to take the earliest boat leaving Inishmore the next day and have time to ride the connecting tour to Clifden.

GALWAY TO ROSSAVEEL (23 MILES)

To leave Galway take **R336 (L100)** following signs to Spiddle or Salthill. It's a bit confusing as you head out of town but once you're on the outskirts there's only one main road heading west along the coast, so it's not difficult to find. The road along the northern shore of Galway Bay has just a few hills and is often nearly eye level with the sea. In 7 miles you pass the tiny village of Furbogh, which marks the beginning of the **Connemara Coast**. This is also the true gateway to the **Gaeltacht** region. The Gaeltacht is the name given to the group of towns and villages that use Gaelic (Irish) as the spoken language. Indeed, the entire region acts as a sort of reservoir for the maintenance and perpetuation of the language. Another important aspect of the Gaeltacht association is the attempt to keep alive Ireland's traditions and culture. On the north Galway Bay coast the Gaeltacht extends as far as Rossaveel, and it also includes the Aran Islands and scattered towns throughout the rest of County Galway.

Evidence that you are in the Gaeltacht abounds as the signs and advertisements increasingly utilize written Irish and fewer English translations. Though many of the people speak Irish, nearly all are bilingual, so you should have no trouble understanding or making yourself understood.

Beyond Furbogh 4 miles (11) is **Spiddle**. Spiddle is the home of *Colaiste Chonnacht*, an Irish summer college that draws people from all over the country to study and produce Irish cultural programs and events. Though fairly small, Spiddle is one of the more populated towns of the Connemara Coast and offers a number of water sports such as kayaking, windsurfing, and sailing. Several **B&Bs** are located in or around Spiddle, and there is an independent **hostel** on the east end of town. There is also a **campground** just a short distance north of Spiddle.

Although many are now roofless, Ireland has an enormous number of ancient stone ruins.

Traveling out of Spiddle on the same level road (**R336**) for 7.5 miles (18.5) and past the village of Inverin, you come to an **IYH hostel**. In another 1 mile (19.5) you approach a fork that goes right to Rossaveel. However, instead of turning, go **straight** down the narrower road, which is a shortcut to the town and the pier. Even if you're not planning a boat trip to the Aran Islands from here, the detour is still worthwhile. The road is a boulder-strewn journey reminiscent of the Burren but quite a bit less hilly. Thatched cottages are more numerous here than in many parts of the island. **Rossaveel** is a sleepy collection of houses, a foodstore, and the Aran Ferry ticket offices. Situated on a tiny finger of water, **Cashla Bay**, this small village is in a nicely sheltered location and is perfect as a departure point to the islands. Turn **left** at the junction just past the foodstore to get to the pier and ticket office. At the office there is a café, as well as picnic tables and public toilets. Total distance to the pier at Rossaveel is 23 miles.

ROSSAVEEL TO INISHMORE

The boat trip to Inishmore takes between twenty and thirty minutes, depending on the weather. Bikes are transported on the ferry for a charge. Try to arrive plenty early so the crew know you have bikes. That way they can be sure to arrange room for them.

Boats from Rossaveel land at Inishmore's largest town and only pier at **Kilronan**. You'll likely be met by men hawking carriage rides around the island, guide service, and bike hire. If you're interested in that sort of thing, all you have to do is look inquisitive and someone will come running. However, if you get off the boat rolling a bicycle, most of the "welcoming committee" will ignore you. Down the pier and around the bay's inlet, the first building you come to is one that houses a combination hostel and pub—quite convenient if you need a place to really unwind.

As far as other services, you need only walk up the hill from the hostel to a fast-food restaurant or around the corner to a foodstore. A souvenir shop is down the hill from the hostel, and a café is just a little way past this. There is also a tourist information office on the same street. In the immediate vicinity, that's about all there is. Across the harbor, past the sandy beach about 1.5 miles, is the other "big" town on Inishmore, **Killeany**.

A bicycle is indisputably the best way to see Inishmore. The majority of the roads (there aren't very many) are smoothly paved and there are very few cars. The ferries coming from Rossaveel and Galway are passengers-only ferries; they are much too small to carry automobiles. About the only vehicles on the island belong to the residents, and they don't seem to be out very often. A breathtakingly scenic route, the northerly road stays mostly near the coastline.

Just at the northwest edge of Kilronan take the right fork marked to Tempall Asurnal. There are numerous spots along this path where houses are few and far between (relatively speaking), and there is a fairly high concentration of thatched houses as well. Clustered with their flock of tiny outbuildings and flanked by a quiltwork of gray stone fences, these homes are about the closest thing you'll ever see to the traditional Irish farmhouse. Except for the power lines, many of these older, whitewashed homes look as if they are remnants of the 1800s, and some probably are.

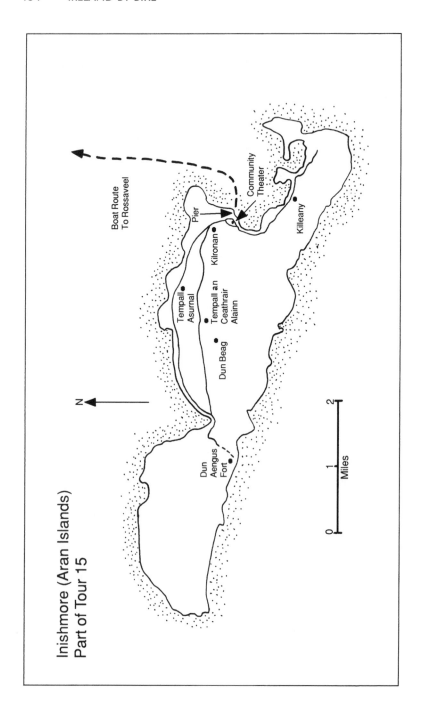

Inishmore (Aran Islands)
Part of Tour 15

N

Boat Route
To Rossaveel

Pier

Community
Theater

Killeany

Kilronan

Tempall
Asurnal

Tempall an
Ceathrair
Alainn

Dun Beag

Dun
Aengus
Fort

Miles
0   1   2

After 4.5 miles along this narrow boreen, turn **left** at the signpost for **Dun Aonghus (Dun Aengus)**. A bit farther down the road, just past the tourist shops, you must dismount and walk the rest of the way, which is approximately fifteen to twenty minutes through sheep pasture and up a moderately sloped hill. Named after Aonghusa, a legendary medieval chief, this prehistoric stone fort is one of the best-preserved, most elaborate structures of its type in all of western Europe. The three concentric rings of the fort cover nearly eleven acres altogether. The outer ring is a well-preserved line of defense consisting of sharp, angular stones placed to act as a barrier to intrusion.

As with so many of Ireland's coastal antiquities, much of Dun Aengus has already been lost to wave erosion. In fact, you can walk unobstructed to the cliff edge. This is quite an exhilarating experience, but you should **observe extreme caution**. There really is nothing but a warning sign to prevent you from going too close to the edge and plunging into the Atlantic. Walk some distance away from the fort and look back at its delicate perch on the sea wall. You will also be able to see the stones scattered around the perimeter to act as a deterrent to invaders. The cliffs, rising about 300 feet, rival or even outdo the Cliffs of Moher. Postcards showing an aerial view of Dun Aengus give you a better idea of just how fantastically the ocean has carved away its precarious position.

Back at the crossroads where you turned to the fort, go **straight** rather than taking the left fork back the way you came. This southerly, more direct route back to Kilronan has additional features along the way. *Tempall an Cheathrair Alainn*, which means "**the Church of the Four Comely Saints**," is not far and off to the **right**. What is left of the small fifteenth-century church is surrounded by a stone enclosure on which four larger stones rest. The saints are buried underneath these stones. Not far from here is **Diarmuid and Grainne's Bed**, a tomb that is over four thousand years old.

Besides the pubs, another engaging way to spend time on the island is to attend the *Man of Aran* movie that is shown in the town hall not far to the west on the edge of Kilronan. The black-and-white movie, produced in 1933, depicts life on Inishmore at the turn of the century. The film used actual islanders to demonstrate the use of the canvas-covered curraghs, shark hunting with harpoons, trying to fish while fighting the awesome Atlantic storms, and hauling seaweed to make enough topsoil to farm the rocky ground. Most remarkable is that the film seems to move from one laborious, dangerous, and difficult task to another. It also depicts the island for what it is, one big rock: rock fences, rock houses, rock everything. Whoever first decided to try to produce crops certainly was optimistic (or very hungry). The town hall, nothing more than a tiny auditorium with a few chairs scattered about the floor, is the perfect setting for showing this classic film of reality and hardship. There is an admission charge. Last showing of the film is late afternoon but check with the tourist office just to make sure.

■ ■

TOUR 16

INISHMORE TO CLIFDEN

Distance: 37 miles
Estimated time: 1 day
Terrain: Moderate to challenging hills

After boating back to Rossaveel from the island of Inishmore, this tour begins a northerly trek into Ireland's Connemara region. On the way to the postcard-perfect town of Clifden the route climbs and descends along the base of a number of inspiring mountain peaks.

CONNECTIONS. Inishmore, one of the three Aran Islands, can be reached by boat from Rossaveel, as described in Tour 15, or from Galway. Air service to Inishmore is also available from Galway on a regular basis.

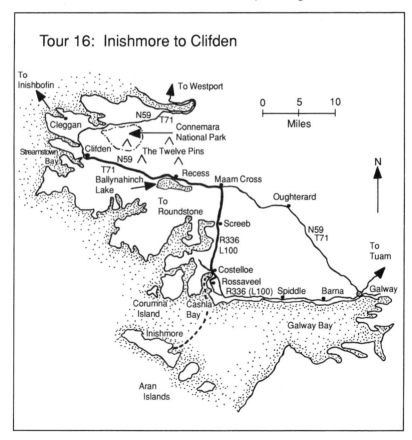

INISHMORE TO CLIFDEN (37 MILES)

Your best bet for completing the mileage from the harbor at Rossaveel to Clifden in one day is to leave Inishmore on the **first available ferry**, which is around 9:00 A.M. That would give you plenty of riding time for this route through Connemara. There aren't very many services along this entire route so you should be sure to stock up on snacks or lunch supplies before leaving Rossaveel.

From the pier at Rossaveel go north on **R336** (**L100**) to Costelloe. In Costelloe, 2 miles away, you leave behind Cashla Bay. Turn **right** at the fork for **R336** to Screeb. For the next 7.5 miles (9.5) the road is level and goes through a barren landscape of bog, boulders, and heather. On the outskirts of Screeb, turn **right** for Maam Cross.

The road continues on flat terrain through the bogs. Fortunately for cyclists, the road only skirts the edge of the nearby mountains. The road is so desolate that you're more likely to see a man cutting and stacking turf than you are to see a house. And the sheep definitely outnumber people by a wide margin. About 5.5 miles from Screeb (15) is Maam Cross. Here there is a store, a restaurant, and a pub. Turn **left** on **N59** to Clifden. After this turn, the road passes alongside the numerous lakes of the **Ballynahinch Fisheries**. In 6.5 miles (21.5) the road begins to climb and roll just a bit, but the terrain is not too difficult. In another 2.5 miles (24) is the village of Recess with a few pubs, a store, and a post office. Of course, the "elementary" thing to do would be to take a break here (a recess in Recess—sorry about that). From here you gently climb up into the surrounding hills. The famous mountains of Connemara, the **Twelve Pins** or **Twelve Bens**, are plainly seen to the right (north). In just over 1 mile (25) you come to a crossroad sporting a heavily loaded signpost. Go **straight** here, but notice the number of signs on the post that indicate a "scenic drive." You really can't go wrong with the Connemara scenery.

In another 4 miles (29), situated on the road overlooking Ballynahinch Lake, is an **IYH hostel** called Ben Lettery. The island in the lake contains the remains of a castle. It is said to have been a prison for captives of the Martin clan who once dominated the area. As the miles toward Clifden progress, the scenery changes as the bogs and heather turn into fragrant pine forests. A final scenic climb through one of these coniferous stands and then a nice downhill run bring you to the town of Clifden (37).

CLIFDEN

Called *An Clochan* (meaning "beehive hut" in Irish), Clifden is situated near the western end of the region but is generally considered to be the capital of Connemara. Perched on an inlet of Clifden Bay, the Owenglin River runs through it as well. It's just as common to see houses or hotels called "Riverview" as it is to see "Bayview."

The land, the sea, and stone combine to form some of Western Ireland's most pastoral settings.

As you enter town, follow the signs to the town center. Because the main street is a one-way running counter to the direction you are entering, turn to the **left** and go 0.25 mile around the block to get to Market Street which has the main row of shops and the tourist office.

Clifden is large enough to have hotels, several B&Bs, three independent hostels, restaurants, shops, **bike rental and repair**, and all the other amenities. At least one of the hostels also offers camping.

Though it is well prepared for a tourist invasion, Clifden still seems to have the heart of a small town. The people eating in the takeout restaurant or walking the aisles of the supermarket all seem to know and to be comfortable with each other. Traditional Irish music plays nearly every night in some of the pubs, but chances are the number of tourists will be significantly smaller than in places such as Killarney or Dingle.

A walk to the north of town leads you to a trail where you can climb the hill to a tremendous panorama of the city. From here you can get a better idea of the layout of the curvy streets below. At the top of the hill is a monument to the founder of the town, John D'Arcy. In fact, if you have seen any tourist brochures of Clifden at all, you will recognize the view from the top of this hill. In addition, if you're a *Quiet Man* fan you will also recognize this as one of the opening shots of the movie, albeit there are a lot more houses and other buildings here now than when the movie was made.

■ ■

TOUR 17
CLIFDEN TO WESTPORT

Distance: 40.5 miles
Estimated time: 1–2 days
Terrain: Lots of climbing at first, interspersed with long descents

The entrance to Connemara National Park lies a few hilly miles from Clifden. After spending time hiking in some of Ireland's most spectacular natural surroundings, the tour takes you to a man-made jewel, Kylemore Abbey. From there you'll find no shortage of peace and solitude as you cycle through the lonely County Mayo backcountry.

CONNECTIONS. Clifden is reached by bike via Tour 16. It is accessible by bus from Galway and from Westport, County Mayo.

CLIFDEN TO LEENANE (22.5 MILES)
From Clifden take **N59 north** out of the city toward Westport. North 1 mile a **campground** sits on the right. The road out is a hilly climb for just over 5 miles, then you begin a rapid 2-mile descent (7), followed by an easy 1.5 miles (8.5) to the outskirts of Letterfrack. This village is sandwiched between the cliffs of **Ballynakilly Harbour** to the north and **Connemara National Park** to the south. Just 0.5 mile farther (9) is the entrance to the park. If you wish to spend some time hiking in the park or would just like more information about it, turn **right at the entrance** and go up the road to the visitors center. There are maps, tourist information pamphlets, an audio-visual presentation, and toilets available here. Hours of the center are 10:00 A.M. to 6:30 P.M. during the tourist season. The park, however, is open year-round.

To continue on to Westport from here **go back** to the park entrance and continue on **N59.** There is an independent hostel just up the road, and the shops and pubs of Letterfrack are found nearby as well. If you are interested in camping in the shadow of the Connemara Mountains or visiting the beaches along the Ballynakilly coast, turn left at the signpost by the pub. There are **two campgrounds** down this road 4 and 5 miles distant. The main road continues straight to Westport/Kylemore Abbey. In just about 1.5 miles (10.5) are a **beautiful waterfall** and a lovely **stone arch bridge.** Look for them off the main road to the left as you round a curve. Cars seem to barely notice the place because of their higher speed, but it should be plainly visible to you on bike. Another 1 mile (11.5), and you come out of the Inagh Valley to the stately, grand **Kylemore Abbey.** Turn **left at the entrance,** which takes you to the parking area, craft and pottery shop, and tearooms.

Built by Mitchell Henry for his wife in the mid-nineteenth century, the

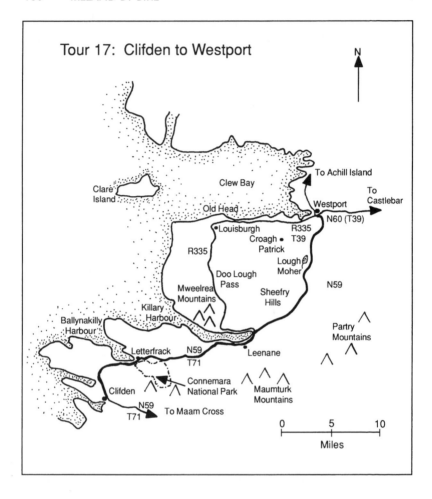

Tour 17: Clifden to Westport

N

To Achill Island

Clew Bay

To Castlebar

Clare Island

Westport

N60 (T39)

Old Head

Louisburgh

R335

Croagh Patrick

T39

R335

Lough Moher

Doo Lough Pass

Mweelrea Mountains

Sheefry Hills

N59

Killary Harbour

Ballynakilly Harbour

Partry Mountains

Letterfrack

N59

Leenane

T71

Connemara National Park

Maumturk Mountains

Clifden

N59

T71

To Maam Cross

0   5   10

Miles

sprawling limestone and Connemara marble estate is now a convent for Benedictine teaching nuns and a girls' school. A series of three lakes stretches past the face of the abbey and extends for some distance along the road in front of it. The most beautiful view of the grounds and the castle is from **Pollacappal Lough**, the lake directly opposite. Set in contrast against the green trees of the **Dorruagh Mountains** in the background, the white of the abbey fairly gleams and its reflection off the lake is truly dazzling.

Down one of the castle's trails is the **Kylemore Gothic Church**, built in the 1870s by Mitchell in memory of his wife. The church has been recently restored, with work beginning in 1992, and visitors are now welcome to tour inside. One admission charge gives you access to the abbey, the church and the surrounding grounds.

In 2.5 miles beyond the abbey (14) you begin the 1-mile-long climb through **Kylemore Pass** (15). Beyond the pass is more desolate, boggy landscape surrounded by the **Twelve Bens** and the **Maumturk Mountains**. For the next 3 miles (18) the terrain continues to change, and you can just begin to glimpse, off in the distance, **Killary Harbour**. In another 1 mile (19), the road meets the coast and you can see down the length of the harbor. Killary is an example of a **fjord**, a U-shaped gorge cut into a valley. Ringed on the north by the **Mweelrea Mountains** and on the south by the **Maumturk Mountains**, Killary's seclusion and shelter within the confines of the mountains make it one of the safest boat harbors in the world.

After 3.5 miles (22.5) along a twisty shoreline road, in a break in the mountains, is the village of Leenane. A movie, *The Field*, was filmed at

Carved and engraved stone crosses are ubiquitous reminders of the past.

least partially in the area; the restaurant at the near edge of town shares the movie's name and displays photographs from the movie inside. The bridge here at the edge of Killary Harbour is pictured several times in the film. There are a number of services here including restaurants and foodstores.

LEENANE TO WESTPORT (18 MILES)

For 2 more miles (24.5) the road stays by the waters of Killary Harbour. Immediately after turning east and away from it you see the sign welcoming you to **County Mayo**. Continue **straight** here on N59.

The road in Mayo begins to take you away from the Maumturk Mountains. However, in Connemara, mountains are not hard to come by and N59 passes down the valley between the **Sheefry Hills** to the north and the **Partry Mountains** to the south and east. Fortunately, the road continues along the base of those mountains and doesn't attempt to go over them. The small azure river that parallels the road for a number of miles is the **Erriff**. Two other rivers, the **Owenduff** and the **Derrycraff**, cross or follow the road from time to time along this lonely stretch.

As is true of many of the Connemara roads, the bogs and sheep become your most common companions. About 10.5 miles from Leenane (35), and soon after you pass **Lough Moher** on the left, you can begin to see in the distance the cone-shaped peak and well-traveled path up the side of Croagh Patrick. Looking toward the northwest from the road, **Croagh Patrick** is the highest mountain in that range. The light-brown scar running along its back is the result of thousands of people making a pilgrimage to the mountain's summit. This trek is described in more detail later in this chapter under Daytrip to Croagh Patrick. From this spot 5.5 miles (40.5), you finally roll into Westport. A **right** at the junction takes you down the steep descent into the town center.

WESTPORT

Westport is one of the most elegantly laid-out towns in all of Ireland. It was originally designed in the late eighteenth century, but the architect is unknown. However, no matter who did the planning, what they left behind combines traces of civility, functionality, and refinement. From the novelty of the town "square" and the grace of the several Georgian houses, to the sylvan aspect of the town's canals, Westport is a unique city.

The road coming in from Leenane takes you directly to **The Octagon**, which serves as the town center. The Octagon is exactly what it sounds like. Instead of an ordinary square, the center is eight-sided with three streets radiating

A row, row, row of boats on the "grounds" of Westport House in County Mayo. The boats can be rented during business hours. Photo by Jeff Kirchhoff

from it. One of them, **James Street**, leads down a block to the **Carrowbeg River**. The first street you come to off James is **South Mall**; on the other side of the river is **North Mall**. The river is tree-lined and its banks are set with stones. The bridges that cross it are arched, and the view from any of the bridges rivals any such scene in the country and possibly in the rest of Europe as well.

The *"i"* is located across the **James Street Bridge** on North Mall. Just to the south is the **post office** and a couple of **banks**. The **railway station** (if you're heading to Dublin from here) is located about 1 mile southeast of the *"i."* The road becomes **Altamount Street** as it heads toward the edge of town. The station is on the right.

Westport does not lack for any type of service. There are at least two **bike shops**, numerous B&Bs, campgrounds, hostels, and a variety of pubs (several of which offer traditional music every night).

The town itself, because of its alluring design, makes for a pleasant stroll. Or for a more structured walk, the tourist office conducts historic tours of the town on certain days of the week during the summer.

Besides the town there are a couple of other interesting sites in the vicinity. **Westport House**, situated at the bottom of a hill just to the west of town on the Louisburgh road, was built in the late 1700s by Westport's Browne family. It was later finished by James Wyatt. Inside are many historical exhibits, a museum, and artifacts from the 1798 Irish rebellion. There is a trail through the woods leading up to the house, and the house is set handsomely on a small lake with a line of rowboats adding a splash of color to the gray walls. The house is open from 10:30 A.M. to 6:00 P.M. Monday through Saturday with reduced hours on Sunday. Admission is charged.

Just northeast of town on Newport Road is the **Anglican Church of Ireland**, which boasts some very fine stonework and a wonderfully constructed spire. Located on South Mall in front of the Catholic church is the **McBride Memorial**, which is a tribute to Major John McBride, an executed leader of the Easter Rising.

DAYTRIP TO CROAGH PATRICK (12 MILES ROUND TRIP)

Croagh Patrick is an angular, pointed peak over 2,500 feet high that dwarfs the surrounding mountains. Legend has it that St. Patrick prayed and fasted for forty days at the top in the year A.D. 441. Another part of the legend suggests that Patrick rang his bell to summon all the snakes in Ireland, and they threw themselves off the mountaintop. The first legend is the one that over 60,000 people a year make the pilgrimage to the top to celebrate. On the last Sunday in July an early morning mass is held at the top, but the rocky path leading up is open year-round. It is an arduous climb and can take several hours to reach the summit, but the views, even if you don't go all the way up, are incomparable. If the weather is clear you can easily see Clare Island and farther across Clew Bay

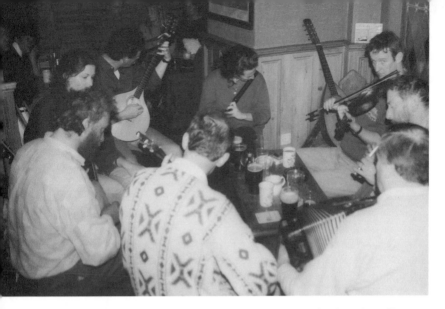

A traditional music session in a Westport, County Mayo pub. Photo by Jeff Kirchhoff

to Achill Island. Perhaps this is the view that inspired William Thackeray to write in 1842, "The islands in the bay which was of gold colour look like so many Dolphins and Whales basking there." Indeed, the low, hummocky islands do look rather like whales. A short distance up the trail is a statue of the saint and a sign giving instructions to the faithful on how to commence the pilgrimage. Please note that the trail gets rather steep at times and you must walk through loose rocks for much of the way. The trail is not recommended if it is raining as the rocks get rather slick.

To get to Croagh Patrick follow **R335 (T39)** out of town to the west to Louisburgh/Croagh Patrick. The road traces Westport Bay, which is part of the larger Clew Bay. To the north you can see the "whales and dolphins" although they are more brilliant from the trail on Croagh Patrick. The road is a relatively easy ride for the 6 miles to the village of Murrisk.

Go through town to the far side where you see a carpark and signpost on the left for the peak. Across the road from the Croagh Patrick entrance is a short ride down to the roofless remains of the fifteenth-century friary called **Murrisk Abbey**. Less than 0.25 mile from the road, it is worth a side trip.

Time (and/or energy) permitting, this daytrip can be extended by continuing on **R335** toward Louisburgh. Beyond Murrisk 4 miles (10) some splendid cliffs loom, as they do beyond the town of Kilsallagh. Beyond Kilsallagh 2 miles (12) is **Old Head**. A trail leads out onto Old Head, from which you can look back at the cliffs and at Croagh Patrick.

If you don't have time or the energy to make the trek in person you can visit Westport's website and take a virtual tour of the pilgrimage up Croagh Patrick. The address is http://www.anu.ie/reek/.

■ ■

TOUR 18
WESTPORT TO BALLINA

Distance: 33 miles
Estimated time: 1 day
Terrain: Relatively flat for most of the distance

Compared to the other tours in this book, this one is of average distance. It seems that for most of this trip's distance water is the predominant theme. Many of the miles involve either following or crossing the numerous lakes of the region. And the tour's final destination is itself situated on a river.

CONNECTIONS. To get to Westport by bike, follow the routes described in Tour 17. Trains from Dublin run to Westport, as do buses. Westport is a trip of about 6 hours by train from Dublin. If you're planning to head back to Dublin soon, Westport is a good place from which to do it. Buses are also available from Galway and Sligo.

WESTPORT TO BALLINA (33 MILES)
Take **N60** out of Westport toward Castlebar. The road is level and smooth. It is not altogether scenic until you get to the village of **Clonkeen** in 6.5 miles. From here the road parallels the shores of the small, but attractive, **Castlebar Lough**, a lake that takes you the additional 4.5 miles (11) to the town of Castlebar.

To find the tourist office as you enter town you must stay on **N60** toward Achill/Belmullet and follow this some distance into town. Then turn **right** at the sign on **Tucker Street**. The *"i"* is just short of two blocks away at the corner with Thomas Street.

Castlebar, located more or less in the center of County Mayo, has a varied and rich history. In fact, its original charter goes back to King James I and was granted in 1613. Also it has been involved in several of the wars that have taken place throughout Ireland's history. In 1798, a small army of French and Irish soldiers beat and routed a superior British force. The resultant quick retreat by the British cavalry led to the event being called "The Races of Castlebar."

Presently, Castlebar is the sight of an Irish Army military barracks. The building in which the **Land League** was founded is in Castlebar. The **Imperial Hotel**, south of the tourist office on **Castle Street**, still has much of the original nineteenth-century paneling and woodwork.

If you have some time to spend, you may be interested in the series of trails or walks that have been set up in and around Castlebar. Maps and brochures about the walks are available at the tourist office. The walks take you out into the lakes and heather-covered hills that surround Castlebar. Designed in cooperation

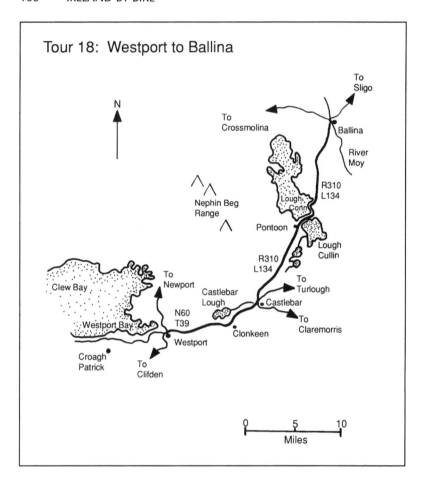

Tour 18: Westport to Ballina

with the International Marching League, these trails are the site of a series of **Four Days' Walks** during certain times of the year. Much like a Volksmarch in the United States, participants receive certificates of fitness for completing one or more of the walks. All of the walks start at either the **Welcome Inn Hotel** on **Newantrim Street** just north of the tourist office or at **Travellers Friend Hotel** on **Mountain View** south of the *"i"* just south of the Post Office.

If you plan to try some of the walks during the day, there are several B&B accommodations available in town, but the nearest campground is 6 miles away. Castlebar has **bike shops**, plenty of pubs, and all other amenities necessary for an overnight stay.

On leaving Castlebar there are two choices of roads at the north end of town that you can take to Ballina. One goes to Turlough, the other to Pontoon. For the more **scenic trip** take the **left fork** on **R310** to Pontoon. This is a very easy ride and in 5.5 miles (16.5) you begin to enter the open, green mountains that are the far southeast edge of the **Nephin Beg Range**. Just 4 more miles (20.5) bring you to the tiny village of Pontoon. There are two small hotels and a pub. Beyond Pontoon 1.5 miles (22) is a bridge that crosses between **Lough Cullin** to the south and the much larger **Lough Conn** to the north. This is a pleasurable lookout point. Just past the bridge is an **independent hostel**.

From the hostel the road follows the shore of Lough Conn for the next 2.5 miles (24.5). Once the road pulls away from the lake, the next 8.5 miles (33) into Ballina are not overly scenic. In fact, the only breathtaking points are the occasional hills as you approach the city.

BALLINA

Ballina is a relatively large town and is the largest in County Mayo. However, it has a small downtown area that is easy to walk around. It sits on the River Moy, which is an internationally acknowledged salmon fishery. It is also home to former Irish President Mary Robinson. There are plenty of pubs, nice shops, restaurants, and at least two **bike shops**. If you happen to be there in July, try to arrrive in town when Ballina is hosting its annual salmon festival which has, of late years, developed into quite an event with music, theater, art, cultural, and heritage events. If you plan to go, however, be sure to reserve lodging well in advance.

Though by Irish standards a comparably young city, Ballina was established in 1723 and was liberated from the British by the same Franco-Irish force that ran the British out of Castlebar. This French influence has led to Ballina being called the capital of French Mayo.

Ballina's location nearly halfway between Westport and Sligo makes it a good place for an overnight stay, particularly if you've had your share of mist and drizzle. There are no cities of any size for the next 38 miles to Sligo.

Follow the Westport road into the town center up to **Garden Stree**t where there is a signpost for the *"i"* to the right. As you travel **south** on Garden it becomes **Tone Street**, and it is lined with a number of restaurants and other shops. As you continue down "the strip," the road continues to be crowded with people and stores as it changes to **Tolan Street** or **Bridge Street**. At the end of this block is where you cross the **River Moy** on the long, many-arched **Ham Bridge**. Following a **left** turn past the bridge, you'll find the tourist office in the first building past **St. Muredach's Cathedral**. This is actually the prettiest part of the city as the two bridges crossing the river are elegant. There will likely be a number of people fishing in or on the banks of the river, and this is a relaxing spot to eat lunch and watch them test their luck. The **post office** is at the top of the hill at the corner of **Casement Street** and **O'Rahilly Street**. The rail station is on the west end of town on the Castlebar/Westport road. You will, no doubt, have noticed it when you came into town.

■ ■

TOUR 19
BALLINA TO SLIGO

Distance: 38 miles
Estimated time: 1 day
Terrain: Relatively flat for most of the miles

For about the first half of this tour you ride through the quiet countryside of County Mayo. As you near the shores of Sligo Bay, mountains begin to loom in the distance and a number of distinct landmarks become apparent. Near the end of the ride traffic picks up considerably and you are advised to watch the road and your mirror instead of the scenery.

CONNECTIONS. By bike, Ballina is reached by taking Tour 18. Train service is available from Galway and Dublin, and buses run regularly from Westport.

BALLINA TO SLIGO (38 MILES)
From Ballina town center take N59 (**L150**) toward Sligo. The road crosses the river at West Bridge before heading northeast out of town. In 3.5 miles you leave Mayo and the west of Ireland and enter into **County Sligo**, the gateway to the northwest. From the border for the next 12.5 miles (16) to the tiny village of Dromore, the road is flat and travels through primarily agricultural lands. There are **very few services** along the way, just an occasional pub and rural post office. Near Dromore you begin to see **Sligo Bay** to the north. Over the next 11 miles (27) to Beltra, the cliffs to the north at **Roskeeragh Point** and the famous flat top peak of **Benbulben Mountain** are visible far off in the distance. The road from Beltra to Ballysadare is 5.5 miles (32.5) along the waters of **Ballysadare Bay**.

The first concentration of anything resembling civilization is at Ballysadare. Because of its position as an important crossroad village, there are a number of shops, restaurants, and pubs. Take **N4** to the **left** and cross the bridge over the mouth of the **Owenmore River** to continue to Sligo. The last 5.5 miles to Sligo (38) are quite a bit **busier**, so you'll have to leave sightseeing behind for awhile as you pedal your way in.

SLIGO
The town of Sligo, the largest in the northwest of Ireland, has a population of just over 20,000 people. Called *Sligeach*, meaning "Place of Shells," the name describes the town's situation at the mouth of the Garavogue River at the inlet of Sligo Harbour. Surrounded by a number of mountain peaks, most notable of which are Benbulben and Knocknarea, the city revolves around its three main

bridges, which cross back and forth over the Garavogue River. People have existed in the Sligo area as far back as 4000 B.C. and possibly earlier. The area figures prominently in history as many battles between Gaelic settlers and Anglo-Norman invaders took place in the surrounding countryside. Finally settled in the mid-thirteenth century by the Anglo-Normans, the region was under more or less local law up to the sixteenth century when many of Cromwell's soldiers were granted lands in and around Sligo and English law prevailed. Sligo received its charter in the early part of the sixteenth century and became a center of brewing, leathermaking, and the production of linen (in which it still specializes). As a result of its never having been walled, several times over the next century Sligo was burned, pillaged, and badly damaged.

One of Sligo's dearest daughters is Countess Markievicz (Constance Gore-Booth), who played an important role in the Easter Rising of 1916. Though she was nearly executed for her trouble, she went on to play a significant part in the eventual formation of the free Irish state.

> *All day I'd looked in the face*
> *What I had hoped 'twould be*
> *To write for my own race*
> *And the reality;*
> *The living men that I hate,*
> *The dead man that I loved,*
> *The craven man in his seat,*
> *The insolent unreproved,*
> *And no knave brought to book*
> *Who has won a drunken cheer,*
> *The witty man and his joke*
> *Aimed at the commonest ear,*
> *The clever man who cries*
> *The catch-cries of the clown,*
> *The beating down of the wise*
> *And great Art beaten down.*

Sligo's most famous son is William Butler Yeats, who immortalized the area in his poems. The one quoted above is called "The Fisherman" and is one of his shorter, but stronger poems. The city bears constant reminders of each of these two distinguished citizens and the surrounding countryside has a variety of monuments to Yeats and his brother, Jack, who painted much of the countryside (not literally, but on canvas). Indeed, the whole countryside is collectively referred to as Yeats Country.

On entering town stay on **N4**, which becomes **Mail Coach Road**. At the **Y** fork for **N4** and **N15/N16**, take the **N4 fork left**. In several blocks this takes you directly to the **tourist office** at the crossroads of **Temple Street** and **Charles**

Street. The **railway/bus station** is three blocks northwest of here at the corner of **Wolf Tone** and **Lord Edwards Street**. The **General Post Office** is on the corner of **Wine Street** and **Quay Street** and is found two long blocks to the east of the rail station. Follow Lord Edwards east until it becomes **Wine Street**.

Sligo town center is oriented primarily around its two main bridges that cross the Garavogue River. One, **Stephen Street Bridge**, running east–west, connects Wine Street with Stephen Street. The other, **Hyde Bridge**, running north–south, connects Thomas Street with Stephen Street.

Several interesting historical attractions are within easy walking distance of Hyde and Stephen bridges. The **City Museum** is found just east of the river on the north side of Stephen Street. The museum is in a building next to the county library. It's a tiny museum with a variety of artifacts ranging from the prehistoric era to the twentieth century. Some of the more interesting things here are the letters and documents written by or about the Countess Markievicz. Of particular note is the arrest summons issued for her in 1920. There is also a display of photos and paintings of the Yeats brothers, especially of W. B. as well as a

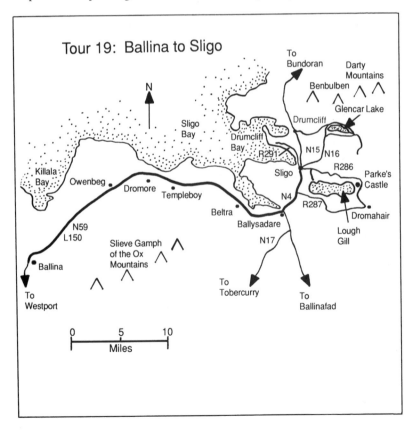

collection of his poems. A number of the photos show his funeral procession as the casket was carried through the streets of the city.

The **Yeats Building**, a fine red-brick structure on the west bank of the river just west of the museum, houses the **Sligo Art Gallery**, which offers to the public a variety of exhibits that change from time to time and hosts an annual Yeats summer school. The **Old Dominican Abbey**, found on Abbey Street just east of Castle Street, includes the fenced remains of the thirteenth-century cloister. Worth taking time to see, it is being reconstructed, and several of its more architecturally valuable windows and arches are still intact. The Abbey is open every day from 9:30 A.M. to 6:30 P.M., from mid-June to mid-September, with guided tours available on request. Telephone 071 46406 for details.

For more information on these and other sights within walking distance in Sligo, the tourist office offers several publications of value, one of which is named *Tourist Trail*. Sligo is an active night town with several pubs offering traditional music almost every night. There is also a cinema that usually offers a choice of several popular films.

DAYTRIP TO LOUGH GILL (28 MILES ROUND TRIP)

A loop around Lough Gill just east of Sligo is a terrific, easy day of cycling. Out of town to the northeast 0.5 mile, take **R286** toward Parke's Castle/Dromahair. In another 1.5 miles (2) turn **right** at the brown "Yeats Country" sign to Hazelwood. In another 1 mile (3) is a carpark at the entrance to the **Hazelwood Sculpture Trail**. Along the trail, which follows the course of Half Moon Bay on Lough Gill, are thirteen unique wood sculptures placed at various intervals. The trail extends for some distance but the most interesting sculptures are found within a few hundred yards of the carpark.

Back at the **main road (4)**, go **right** toward the castle. In 1 mile (5) go **right** at the signpost for "Lough Gill Loop." This is a 1-mile (6) diversion that gives you a bird's-eye view of the lake that you won't get to see from anywhere else on the loop. This road winds back to the main road where you **turn once again** for Parke's Castle. In 5.5 miles (11.5), just 0.5 mile after entering County Leitrim, is **Parke's Castle**.

The castle, which is rooted on the shores of Lough Gill, is actually a seventeenth-century plantation that was once given as payment to one of Oliver Cromwell's soldiers. Today the castle is surrounded by stone walls with well-restored towers at the corners. Local craftsmen rebuilt the wooden inner structures of the castle using only wood pegs and notched wood beams. For a small admission you get a guided tour of the inside rooms and courtyard. Inside you can view an audio-visual production explaining not only the history of the castle but also several other ancient features nearby and in other counties. Summer opening hours are from 9:30 A.M. to 6:30 P.M.

From the castle continue 4.5 miles (16) to Dromahair. On the way you

Carvings and elaborate arches attest to the skill of former artisans.

pass back into County Sligo. Just before town is a sign to the **right** for **Creevylea Abbey**. These remains date to the early 1500s and are of a Franciscan friary founded by the O'Rourke family. **Return** to the turnoff and continue into **Dromahair**, where there is a foodstore, pubs, a restaurant, post office, and pay phone. Beyond Dromahair are several places to picnic, so this is a good spot to pick up supplies.

Outside of town 0.5 mile (16.5) turn **right** on the road to Sligo. The road winds its way through what is called "Wild Rose Country," but it's not plainly visible why it's called this. In 7 more miles (23.5) there is a parking area marked **Dooney Rock**. There is a forest walk here that will take you to the lakeshore. In 2.5 miles (26) you arrive at the junction with **N4**. Turn **right** here and continue the 2 miles (28) back into Sligo.

DAYTRIP TO GLENCAR LAKE AND WATERFALL (20 MILES ROUND TRIP)

Take **N16** to the northeast out of Sligo toward Enniskillen. In just over 4 miles, turn **left** at the sign for Glencar. Follow this road as it makes its way along the northern shore of Glencar Lake. It is a beautiful ride along the base of the **Dartry Mountains**, which surround the entire lake. In 3 miles (7) you come to a **pulloff** marked "Glencar Waterfall." There are toilets here and a place to picnic.

Climb the marked stone path up to the waterfall, which drops from the cliff nearly 50 feet. Ferns, mosses, and other greenery surround this largely unspoiled spot to relax. Yeats's poem "The Stolen Child" was inspired by the waterfall, which is actually the last of a series of waterfalls that start higher up the mountain.

Back at the carpark there is an impressive view back to the west of the towering peak of **Kieve Mountain**. **Retrace** your path back to Sligo for a total distance of 14 miles, or continue 3 more miles around the lake, then join back with **N16** to return to town for a total distance of 20 miles.

■ ■

TOUR 20
SLIGO TO DONEGAL

Distance: 43.5 miles
Estimated time: 1–2 days
Terrain: Flat to moderately hilly

You can't go very far on this tour before coming to another set of historically or archaeologically important sites or ruins. You can also enjoy a number of miles where the road hugs the shore of Donegal Bay. Traffic is reasonably light except on the approaches to the towns of Bundoran and Ballyshannon.

CONNECTIONS. Bicycle tourists can reach Sligo by completing Tour 19. Air service to Sligo is available from either Shannon or Dublin, and trains also run to Sligo from Dublin. Buses originating in Ballina and Westport also travel to Sligo.

SLIGO TO DONEGAL (43.5 MILES)

Head north to Donegal by getting on **N15** in Sligo. The road quickly takes you away from the traffic and bustle of Sligo. Down the road 5 miles is **Drumcliff Church** and **cemetery** where W. B. Yeats was buried in 1948. Poetically laid out near the base of the mountain **Benbulben**, the site of his resting place was picked according to Yeats's wishes and the epitaph was self-written, "Cast a cold eye on life, on death, Horseman pass by."

Also here is an exquisitely carved **stone cross** dating to the eleventh century. The east face of the cross features scenes from the Old Testament, and the west face has illustrations from the New. Reportedly, the cross is one of the most unusual in the entire country. **Across the road** are the remains of an ancient round tower built sometime between A.D. 900–1200.

A couple hundred yards up the road take a **left** at the sign to Lissadell House. In 4 miles (9) down this rather narrow road, turn **left** again at another Lissadell sign. The house is down this lane another 0.5 mile. Once the home of the famous arctic explorer Henry Gore-Booth and his family, including Constance (Countess Markievicz), today the house is open to the public as a showcase of antiques, crafts, and the way of life in the 1800s. The grounds around the house are part of a Forestry and Wildlife Bird Reserve, and two or three trails traverse the woods. The house and grounds are open from the first of June until mid-September and there is an admission charge.

Back at the entrance go **straight** across the road following the brown **"Yeats Country"** sign. In 2.5 miles (12) this small road meets the main road (**N15**). At Grange, which is 2.5 miles farther (14.5), you will find your best opportunity to look seaward and see the tiny isle of **Inishmurray**, an island that has been devoid

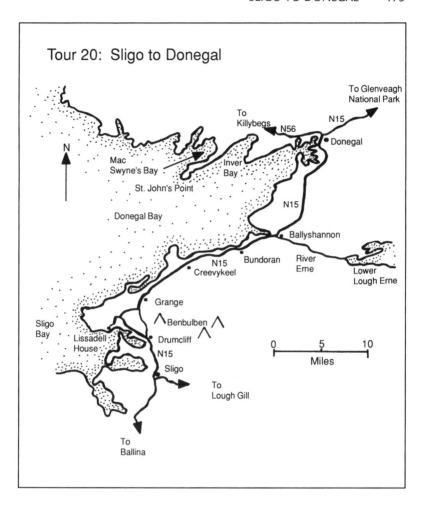

Tour 20: Sligo to Donegal

Continuing north on **N15** the road maintains its bearing along the coast in sight and smell of the bay. For a short distance more you remain in County Sligo, but 3.5 miles (22) from Creevykeel you enter into **County Leitrim**. As is the case of the trip to Lough Gill where you briefly enter County Leitrim, the

of anything but stone ruins since 1947. After Grange the road follows a direct line along the shore of **Donegal Bay** for 4 miles (18.5) to a carpark on the **right** for **Creevykeel Court Tomb**. This unique structure was constructed around five thousand years ago by early Stone Age farmers. Though the tomb is now without a roof, there are two main circles of stone that apparently served as burial chambers. These are flanked by an entryway that probably served as a court for ritual ceremonies.

stay here is short, including only 3.5 miles (25.5) and one tiny village, Tullaghan. Now the road enters **County Donegal**.

Just after entering the county you'll reach **Bundoran**, a nicely situated seaside resort town on Donegal Bay. At the near edge of town there are signs indicating a **cliff walk**. If you're stopping here for the day, the well-traveled path is worth visiting. Farther in, the **tourist office** is found on the seaward side of the road right before reaching the sign to the beach. Located nearby are public toilets. Bundoran offers a variety of amenities commensurate with its status as a holiday stop for vacationing Irish families. And there is a **bike shop** here as well.

Through Bundoran keep following the signs for **N15** and in 4 miles (29.5) you come to **Ballyshannon** where you will pass an independent hostel and a sign for camping. Ballyshannon is also a popular vacation spot, although it is not as nicely situated on the coast as Bundoran. It is, however, perched above the River Erne near the point where the river empties into the bay. Historically Ballyshannon was an important point of commerce and military significance because of its lofty station above the river. The O'Donnell family, of which the famous Red Hugh O'Donnell was a member, laid claim to this land for several centuries.

Remain on **N15** as the road curves its way through town until you climb the final hill and head out of town. For the next 9 miles (38.5) the highway pulls away from the coast and is considerably less scenic. One consolation is the wide shoulder, which gives cars plenty of room to zoom by.

Working its way ever closer to the wrinkled Donegal Bay coast, in 4.5 miles (43) the road brings you to the Donegal **tourist office** just before you actually reach Donegal town. Just west of the *"i"* is a trail leading to a fifteenth-century Franciscan friary known as **Donegal Abbey**. Though not in very good repair, the friary is a rather famous one in Irish history and members of the O'Donnell family, who founded the abbey, are buried here. Down the road 0.5 mile farther (43.5) is Donegal town center.

DONEGAL

Donegal sits at the junction of the River Eske and a tongue of Donegal Bay and "as the crow flies" is only 8 miles from the Northern Ireland border. The town is laid out around "The Diamond," which isn't a diamond but a triangle. Roads come off the triangle from all three points. To the south is the Bundoran road (**N15**), to the northeast the continuation of **N15** (and the most direct route to a Northern Ireland border crossing), and to the west **N56**.

All types of shops, restaurants, and pubs are available, and many can be found within easy walking distance down any of the roads coming off the Diamond. **Bike repair** is available nearby, and the **post office** is found just north of the easily located Donegal Castle. Donegal also offers a *An Oige* hostel and several

Now roofless, these stone circles near Sligo were used around 3000 B.C. to bury the dead of local families. Photo by Jeff Kirchhoff

independent hostels as well as B&Bs. Camping is available at at least one of the hostels. Telephone prefix is 073.

As you come into the town look to the left to see the Quay Walk next to the river. Following this around to the west takes you to the old **Franciscan abbey** which was created in the fifteenth century by Red Hugh O'Donnell. The abbey is in ruins now, but is situated nicely along the lake. *The Annals of the Four Masters*, a famous historical account of Ireland, was created in the seventeenth century by four monks who lived at the abbey. The obelisk in the center of the Diamond was built in remembrance of these Four Masters.

A bit farther up the road is the old quay and an anchor dating from Napoleonic times. The *"i"* is also located nearby.

Donegal town gets its name from *Dun na gall*, which means "Fort of the Foreigners" and refers to the fact that the Vikings established a fort here in the tenth century. The castle that remains today sits just north of the Diamond and comprises several buildings from the sixteenth and seventeenth centuries.

Just over the bridge crossing the river and leading to the west of town is a well laid-out walk along the river called the **Drumcliffe** or **Bank Walk**. It follows the river south until it comes opposite the Franciscan friary you saw from the tourist office. You also have a panoramic view back toward the whole city from the bend in the river.

■ ■

TOUR 21

DONEGAL TO GLENCOLUMBKILLE

Distance: 36 miles
Estimated time: 1 day
Terrain: Relatively flat during the first half, becoming
moderately to very hilly

Like so many of the other tours in this book, this one follows the coastline. This is where similarities end, though. No other part of Ireland better depicts the raw, natural beauty of the island. The entire length of this trip is a procession of cliffs, coastal vistas, and desolate bogland. This is truly Ireland's wild country.

CONNECTIONS. By bike it is best to reach Donegal by following Tour 20. The second-best connection to the city is by bus from Sligo.

DONEGAL

In Ireland, the name "Donegal" brings to mind a rugged, wild country, and in this tour the hauntingly beautiful southern coast of County Donegal is explored. The erosive forces of ice and water have been the main contributors in shaping the rocky terrain. With all but one point on the compass within its grasp, the sea has pounded, torn, and pulled at the northern, southern, and

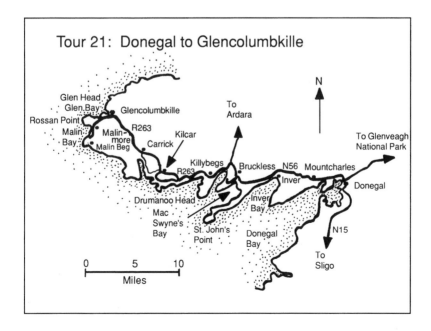

Tour 21: Donegal to Glencolumbkille

western coastlines. And what the sea can't reach, glaciers did in the last ice age. Much of the poor, rocky soil of today has its origin in the meltwaters of ancient ice flows. The low, potholed valleys created by glacial action became the ever-present bogs as the ice melted and retreated.

The land and the hard life it provides have developed the rugged character of its citizens too. It is here that the greatest effort has been made to preserve the Irish language. In fact, County Donegal contains a greater number of Irish speakers than any other county in the country. Perhaps this is testament to the independence and traditional values one develops in such a coarse, stony world.

All books must have a place to end and this one ends with Tour 21 at Glencolumbkille. Depending on the amount of time you have left in your trip and what types of things you would like to see, there are at least a couple of options for what to do next. One is to simply ride back to Donegal and then get a bus to your next destination. While this may work for one or two people with single bikes, it won't work for those with tandems or for large groups. Buses simply can't accommodate more than two bikes.

For those with more time, consider cycling up the coast from Glenco-lumbkille, over to Glenveagh National Park and then east to Letterkenny, continuing on farther and crossing into Northern Ireland.

DONEGAL TO GLENCOLUMBKILLE (36 MILES)

At the diamond go **left** over the bridge crossing the River Eske and con-tinue west on **N56**. In 2 miles the road nearly intersects the bay and in 2 more miles (4) you come to the village of Mountcharles. The most prominent build-ing in town, "The Hall," once owned by Lord Mountcharles (who also obvi-ously built the town), is a very fine example of Georgian architecture. Turn **left** on any of the streets in town to get a view of the coves and inlets of Donegal Bay, which Mountcharles impressively watches over.

Stay on **N56** and follow the route to Killybegs. **Inver Bay** is the next finger of water protruding into the coast, and you come upon it in another 4 miles (8). Dunkineely is the next town and is 3.5 miles (11.5) beyond Inver Bay. Just beyond Dunkineely is a road to the **left** to **St. John's Point**. The point is actually 4 miles away but about 1 mile (12.5) down this road offers a choice view of **MacSwyne's Bay** and across the water to **Drumanoo Head**. You can choose to follow the detour and go the remaining 3 miles to the lighthouse at the tip of this thin peninsula or turn here and go back to the main road (13.5—not counting a ride to the point).

Back at **N56** go left toward Killybegs. In 1 mile (14.5) pass through the small village of **Bruckless**. The first real taste of climbing starts here, and there are some fast descents just beyond town. For 2 miles (16.5) the road bends north and away from the coast. N56 forks right but you should **continue straight on R263**. This road then bends back to the south again. A mile outside

Killybegs (17.5) is an independent hostel on the right. Killybegs (18.5) is a true fishing village, as evidenced by the overwhelming *eau de poisson* that pervades the air as you enter town. Closer to the town center is a jumble of shops lining the narrow streets, and most types of services are available here.

Carry on through Killybegs on **R263** to the west. Beyond town 1.5 miles (20) is a very good beach on the inside curve of the bay. The way is well marked. **Another entrance** is 1 mile farther (21). Across the bay from here you can get a fantastic look at Benbulben's majestic facade standing tall across the bay in Sligo. For another 1 mile (22) the road twists and climbs its way along the coast. Here there is a parking area with picnic tables and a good place to pull over and take a look at **Fintragh Bay**, which the road is following. From here you can also look back at the strand (beach) you passed not far back. The surrounding green headlands are used primarily for pasture and hay and, again, the fields extend right up to the rocky cliff.

The road does some more climbing and descending for the next 3 miles (25) and then finishes with a **steep descent** the last 1 mile (26) into the town of **Kilcar**. The well-known **Studio Donegal**, a handweaving operation that

In many places, "turf," peat bog used for home fires, is still cut by hand and stacked to dry on the roadside.

produces a wide variety of earthy tweeds, is nestled at the bottom of the hill just before the road begins to climb again. Through Kilcar follow the narrower, but more scenic **coast road** rather than staying on R263. The coast road adds little, if any, distance to the overall trip and is much more pleasant since it gets right into the heart of the Donegal seaboard. *Note:* Because this road is considerably narrow, curvy, and steep, I recommend not taking this route in rainy or foggy weather. Instead, stay on **R263** toward **Carrick.**

In another 1.5 miles (27.5) you pass an independent hostel and 1.5 miles beyond that (29) the coastal road intersects again with **R263**. This becomes the main avenue into Carrick, which is only 1 mile away (30). Carrick offers a foodstore, a couple of pubs, and an independent hostel.

In Carrick proceed on the road with signs to Glencolumbkille. The route now leads through the verdant, heather-covered hills and takes you away from the bay. The mountains become a darker, richer green and the white sheep stand in more contrast on the hillsides. The foothills are quite boggy and a lot of peat is cut from here. For 5.5 miles (35.5) you traverse moderate to sometimes challenging hills as you progress to the hill overlooking the town of Glencolumbkille. Just before heading down the hill **turn left** at the pulloff for the sweeping panorama overlooking Glencolumbkille village and the resplendent crags and cliffs of this extreme western tip of the county. Out in front are the crashing waves and misty lands of **Rossan Point**, while farther north are the bluffs along **Glen Head**. Back at the road go **left** for the town, which is just down the hill 0.5 mile (36).

GLENCOLUMBKILLE

This is one of the smallest and, by far, the most remote of all of the tour destinations. The name, meaning "Valley of St. Colmcille," refers to the sixth-century saint who, for at least part of his life, lived here. In town there is an authentically built **Folk Village** consisting of a number of thatched cottages. Inside each one, a different aspect of traditional Irish life from the seventeenth to nineteenth centuries is depicted. In addition, there is an old schoolhouse and a country pub. The admission charge is reasonable, so this is a worthwhile diversion from cycling and seeing the countryside.

Though at first glance the Glencolumbkille area seems to be isolated from civilization, that impression is not completely accurate. A number of tourists find their way here so there are plenty of accommodations available. In fact, you may find yourself wondering how so many lodgings stay in business. There's nowhere near the number that, say, Dingle has, but you should have no trouble finding a place to stay.

The primary reason people come to this outlying region is for the landscape. Riding out to Rossan Point, which overlooks both **Glen Bay** and **Malin Bay**, is a remarkable study in contrast. First, there is the ever-present green of

Ireland's history is preserved in countless artifacts of its past.

the hills, dotted with gray, lichen-covered stones and tinged with tiny yellow flowers daring to show their faces. Then there is the sky, sometimes brilliant blue and at other times a somber, ashen color. The face of the mountains changes with the clouds and can instantaneously transform from callous, black shadows into dazzling emerald peaks. And the sea, always known to be fickle, rhythmically fades and deepens in color as the waves tirelessly pound the shore. Set among this wild natural beauty are the stone ruins and relics of a past that stretches back more than five thousand years.

Within town, there are a couple of archaeologically important remains, but most are outside the city limits. Pick up a detailed map at the small, but informative, tourist office for more information. The *"i"* is located among several shops on the left side of the road as you enter town. On the grounds of the **Church of Ireland** there is a finely carved stone cross and a Stone Age gravestone. A number of other ruins can be found by following the road west out of town past the folk village.

This outstanding coastal road merits the added mileage because of its exceptional seascapes, but there are a couple of stone artifacts here as well. Beyond town 3.5 miles, just past the **Glencolumbkille Hotel**, take a **sharp left**. Go down the narrow road for nearly 1.5 miles to the pulloff at **Glenmalin Court Cairn**. Other remnants of Ireland's ancient past can be found by going back to the hotel turnoff and **going left**. This road continues until finally ending at the outpost village of **Malinmore**.

FOR REFERENCE AND READING

Irish Tourist Board headquarters are located in Dublin, but in the United States write to 345 Park Avenue, New York, NY 10154 or call 212/418-0800 to obtain any of the following publications. The Tourist Board will send you copies of anything you request that is available at no charge, as well as an order form for the rest of its publications.

Irish Tourist Board Offices. Specifies opening times and location of each *Bord Failte* office.

County Guides. Each is forty to fifty pages and describes the sights and scenery in one of the counties. Just order the one you'll need for your county of arrival. Others can be obtained from *Bord Failte* offices along the way.

Irish Tourist Board Approved Accommodations. A complete sourcebook of all lodging approved by the Irish Tourist Board (ITB) in the twenty-six counties of the Republic of Ireland. This is a rather large book and may be too big to tote in your panniers. You could photocopy appropriate pages before you go, however.

Town & Country Homes Association Guest Accommodations. Lists B&Bs in all twenty-six counties that are members of the association. This narrows down the choices considerably and makes the book small enough to fit in packs. Includes prices, location, number of rooms, discounts for children, and other useful information. The book also includes a small black-and-white photo of each home. All Town and Country Homes are ITB approved.

Irish Youth Hostel Association Handbook. Describes location, price, and services of all forty-three IYH (*An Oige*) hostels in Ireland. All IYH hostels are approved by the Irish Tourist Board.

The Guinness Guide. A guide to 150 Independent Holiday Hostels found throughout the country. No membership is required at these hostels.

Ireland Self-Catering Guide. Lists over eighteen hundred houses, cottages, farmhouses, apartments, and castles that are available for rental by the week or longer. Self-catered lodgings include facilities for cooking, laundering, and several other amenities and are perfect for groups. They are ideal if you are sightseeing in one area for an extended time.

Calendar of Events. A guide for locating horse races, festivals, cultural exhibits, and sporting events throughout the country.

IRISH INTEREST WEBSITES

Because the World Wide Web is an ever-changing place, it is quite possible that some of these sites will no longer be active when you view them. Also, unless the site is an "official" site you should not necessarily rely on the accuracy of the information. Always double check any dubious claims and do not accept them at face value. That said, the web can provide enormous detail about Ireland without your having to take the time to send requests by postal mail. Many of these pages have links to other Irish sites so once you begin you are likely to come away with loads of information. *Note:* All of the addresses listed begin with http:// although with many web browsers you do not have to type that portion.

BOOKS

www.irishbooks.com/books.html

FOLK SONG LYRICS

ameba.lpt.fi/~zaphod/irish

GENERAL INTEREST

larkspirit.com/general/irishhub.html

home.iol.ie/1/

www.browseireland.com/

HISTORY

wwwvms.utexas.edu/~jdana/irehist.html

LODGING

An Oige Youth Hostels: www.commerce.ie/anoige

Independent Holiday Hostels: www.iol.ie/hostel

Independent Hostel Owners: www.epcmedia.net/ihi/

Searchable Hotel/Inn Listings: ireland.iol.ie/be-our-guest/

Town & Country Homes: www.commerce.ie/towns_and_country/

NEWS AND INFORMATION

Irish Times: www.irish-times.com/

RTE Online: www.rte.ie/index.html

PASSPORT INFORMATION

http://travel.state.gov/passport_services.html

TOURISM

Dublin Tourism: www.visit.ie/countries/ie/dublin/index.html

Irish Tourist Board: www.ireland.travel.ie/home/index.asp

www.irish-insight.com/

www.tour-ireland.com/

www.shamrock.org/

www.touchtel.ie/

www.netc.ie/tourism.html

www.goireland.ie/visitorsguide/

www.anu.ie/westport/ — Pages can be viewed in Irish (Gaelic)

www.westclare.com

ireland.iol.ie/kerry-insight

www.kerrygems.ie/index/

CURRENCY EXCHANGE

Exchange rate in dollars per pound	£1	£2	£3	£4	£5	£6	£7	£8	£9
$1.40	1.40	2.80	4.20	5.60	7.00	8.40	9.80	11.20	12.60
$1.45	1.45	2.90	4.35	5.80	7.25	8.70	10.15	11.60	13.05
$1.50	1.50	3.00	4.50	6.00	7.50	9.00	10.50	12.00	13.50
$1.55	1.55	3.10	4.65	6.20	7.75	9.30	10.85	12.40	13.95
$1.60	1.60	3.20	4.80	6.40	8.00	9.60	11.20	12.80	14.40
$1.65	1.65	3.30	4.95	6.60	8.25	9.90	11.55	13.20	14.85
$1.70	1.70	3.40	5.10	6.80	8.50	10.20	11.90	13.60	15.30
$1.75	1.75	3.50	5.25	7.00	8.75	10.50	12.25	14.00	15.75
$1.80	1.80	3.60	5.40	7.20	9.00	10.80	12.60	14.40	16.20
$1.85	1.85	3.70	5.55	7.40	9.25	11.10	12.95	14.80	16.65

SUMMARY OF TYPICAL PRICES IN 1998

The exchange rate in 1998 was approximately US$1.55/£1. Multiply each of the figures below by this amount or see Appendix 2 for quick reference for other exchange rates. All prices listed below are in Irish pounds.

Bike Rental for one day/week	7.00/30.00
(additional charges apply for one-way rentals)	
One night in B&B for one person/sharing	14.00–16.00
One night in Independent Holiday Hostel	7.00
Car hire for one day (unlimited mileage)	35.00
One week in self-catered lodging	300.00
Train ticket across country (passenger & bike)	16.00–18.00
Pint of Guinness Stout in a pub	1.90
Liter of milk	.65
Inner tube	2.75
Can of carbonated beverage	.50–.75
Fish and chips from a takeout restaurant	3.50
Liter of gasoline	.70
Siamsa Tire ticket	8.00
Entrance to extensively renovated ruins	3.00–5.00
Entrance to less extensively renovated ruins	1.00–1.50

ABOUT THE AUTHOR

Robin Krause's first glimpse of Ireland came as his boat landed in Rosslare Harbour on Ireland's southeast coast. An avid traveler, he had never bicycled in a foreign country, but his wife Kelly (pictured) encouraged a two-wheeled return trip to Ireland. Although hesitant to call a vacation in Ireland "research," their most recent trip marks their third extensive cycling trip to the Emerald Isle. Robin and his wife have also backpacked frequently in western Europe and the interior of Mexico, and are currently planning travels in the northeastern United States and Canada with their two sons Joel (left) and Conor.

Photo by Jeff Kirchhoff

THE MOUNTAINEERS, founded in 1906, is a nonprofit outdoor activity and conservation club, whose mission is "to explore, study, preserve, and enjoy the natural beauty of the outdoors. . . . " Based in Seattle, Washington, the club is now the third-largest such organization in the United States, with 15,000 members and five branches throughout Washington State.

The Mountaineers sponsors both classes and year-round outdoor activities in the Pacific Northwest, which include hiking, mountain climbing, ski-touring, snowshoeing, bicycling, camping, kayaking and canoeing, nature study, sailing, and adventure travel. The club's conservation division supports environmental causes through educational activities, sponsoring legislation, and presenting informational programs. All club activities are led by skilled, experienced volunteers, who are dedicated to promoting safe and responsible enjoyment and preservation of the outdoors.

If you would like to participate in these organized outdoor activities or the club's programs, consider a membership in The Mountaineers. For information and an application, write or call The Mountaineers, Club Headquarters, 300 Third Avenue West, Seattle, Washington 98119; (206) 284-6310.

The Mountaineers Books, an active, nonprofit publishing program of the club, produces guidebooks, instructional texts, historical works, natural history guides, and works on environmental conservation. All books produced by The Mountaineers are aimed at fulfilling the club's mission.

Send or call for our catalog of more than 300 outdoor titles:

The Mountaineers Books
1001 SW Klickitat Way, Suite 201
Seattle, WA 98134
1-800-553-4453
e-mail: mbooks@mountaineers.org
website: www.mountaineers.org

Other titles you may enjoy from The Mountaineers:

BY BIKE™ SERIES:
    EUROPE BY BIKE™: 18 Tours Geared for Discovery, Second Edition,
        Karen & Terry Whitehill
    ENGLAND BY BIKE™: 18 Tours Geared for Discovery, *Les Woodland*
    FRANCE BY BIKE™: 14 Tours Geared for Discovery, *Karen & Terry Whitehill*
    GERMANY BY BIKE™: 20 Tours Geared for Discovery, *Nadine Slavinski*
plus **CHINA BY BIKE™, HAWAII BY BIKE™, LATIN AMERICA BY BIKE™,
NEW ZEALAND BY BIKE™,** and **NOVA SCOTIA & THE MARITIMES BY BIKE™**
Popular series giving all the essentials of bicycling throughout the world, with tips on planning, safety, health, food, accommodations, sites of interest, buying and outfitting a bike, and more.

**CONDITIONING FOR OUTDOOR FITNESS: A Comprehensive Training
Guide,** *David Musnick, M.D. & Sandy Elliot, Editors*
The most comprehensive guide to conditioning, fitness, and training for all outdoor activities, written by a team of sports fitness experts. Offers "whole body" training programs for hiking, biking, skiing, climbing, paddling, and more.

**WILDERNESS NAVIGATION: Finding Your Way Using Map, Compass,
Altimeter, & GPS,** *Bob Burns & Mike Burns*
An essential how-to covering the tools of orientation, navigation, and routefinding, and the skills for using those tools. Includes the basics of how to read a map; distance and slope measurement; customizing and modifying maps; magnetic declination; positioning; how to use altimeters and GPS receivers; wilderness routefinding; and more.

**MOUNTAIN BIKE ADVENTURES IN SOUTHWEST BRITISH COLUMBIA:
50 Rides,** *Greg Mauer*
50 classic rides throughout seven key regions of southwest B.C. Includes daytrips and overnighters for all skill levels on all types of terrain, from paved roads to primitive backcountry roads, to double and single tracks.

BICYCLING WITH CHILDREN: A Complete How-To Guide, *Trudy Bell*
A thorough and readable manual for active families wanting to develop solid biking skills for a lifetime of fun. Answers real questions from real parents, covering infants to teens.

BICYCLE GEARING, *Dick Marr*
A complete guide to gearing and shifting strategies.

**BACKPACKER'S MAKING CAMP: A Complete Guide for Hikers, Mountain
Bikers, Paddlers & Skiers,** *Steve Howe, Alan Kesselheim, Dennis Coello, John Harlin*
A comprehensive, four-season camping how-to compiled by *BACKPACKER* magazine field experts for anyone traveling by foot, boat, bicycle, or skis, through all kinds of terrain, year-round.